Joy Adamson

THE
SEARCHING
SPIRIT

An Autobiography

With a Foreword by
ELSPETH HUXLEY

COLLINS and HARVILL PRESS
London, 1978

ISBN 0 00 216035 8

Made and printed in Great Britain by
William Collins Sons & Co. Ltd, Glasgow
for Collins, St. James's Place and
Harvill Press, 30A Pavilion Road, London SW1

To Oma and Elsa

Acknowledgements

In writing this book I have received much help from my publishers, initially from the late Sir William Collins and subsequently from Marjorie Villiers, Adrian House and Ernestine Novak, and I would like to express my gratitude.

Contents

Illustrations

Colour

Black and white

Foreword

Joy Adamson is a pioneer. Not in the old sense of covered wagons, outspans and axes – although much of her life has been spent in wild, rough places about as far as you can get from big cities – but in the sense of one who leads towards new ways of looking at our surroundings, and towards a better understanding of the fellow creatures with whom we share our world.

This is a large claim, which Joy Adamson would be the last to make for herself; she is not a scientist, philosopher or thinker, but one who goes out and does things, not to prove a theory but from the dictates of her heart. The most famous thing she did was to rear an orphaned lion cub, as many have done before her; but then, when the cub grew to maturity, instead of sending it to a zoo, at the expense of endless care and patience to return the lioness to the wilds whence she came. The remarkable part of the story was that, when Elsa had mated with a truly wild lion, she led her litter of cubs back to George and Joy Adamson's camp, as it were introduced them, and for the rest of her life continued to re-visit her foster-parents at intervals, and to regard them as trusted friends.

The success of this experiment, and of a subsequent association with a cheetah, knocked on the head several generally accepted beliefs. That a wild animal, once tamed, will never be accepted back by its fellows, or be able to survive without human protection; that a once-tamed predator such as a lion can never be trusted not to 'turn nasty' and must always be confined; in essence, that the gulf between beasts in the wild and human beings must be guarded always by a man with a gun. Perhaps it went deeper than that. Perhaps the extraordinary grip the Elsa story took upon its readers was due to its evocation of one of mankind's oldest myths, or dreams: of a Golden Age of harmony when the lion lay down with the lamb, before Adam took his fatal bite of the apple.

No one, I suppose, really believed that this dream-world could be re-created on our ravaged planet; but the episode showed that, in very special circumstances, the fear and guilt normally governing the relations between man and wild beast could be overcome. Basically, the Elsa story is a love story. Joy loved Elsa, Elsa trusted Joy in return; and that hoary old adage, love conquers all, was proved, in this unexpected context, to be true. Love conquered fear, that deep instinctive fear that man and lion have felt for each other ever since man came down from the trees.

Elsa's story has been fully told; now Joy turns to her own. Her life did not begin and end with Elsa. If the famous lioness had never entered her life, she would have been known, if not to so wide a circle, as a painter of distinction, especially as a botanical painter. Her drawings of East African plants and wild flowers are classics of their kind. Her most ambitious project was to complete a large series of portraits of men and women of the many tribes and sub-tribes of Kenya, each in the full regalia of his or her people. Even when she made these paintings, some thirty years ago, much of the regalia had been discarded and forgotten, and had to be extracted from the recesses of smoke-darkened huts; by now, or at best in a few years, the shields and head-dresses, ornaments and anklets, will have disintegrated, and, unless examples are preserved in museums, her paintings may be the only record of these past barbaric glories to survive.

By this time, Joy was committed to the cause which has since engaged all her passionate energies: the attempt to keep in being all that is possible of the natural splendours of Africa. These are threatened from every side. Forests are melting away, bush turning into deserts, indigenous plants disappearing, species after species of the marvellous fauna being placed on an 'endangered list' of creatures dwindling towards the point of no return. It is a stark prospect. Of the small and dedicated band of those who are trying to stem the tide, Joy is outstanding. Every penny of the money she has made from her books has gone to the Elsa Wild Animal Appeal, to be spent on ways and means of protecting and studying wildlife all over the world.

No one who reads these pages will question Joy's physical courage. Leopards and lions of the bush have been her playmates. Moreover, her husband's job as Game Warden entailed hunting and destroying man-eating lions, and more than once she found herself too close for comfort to these leonine delinquents. Yet possibly the bravest thing she did was to walk on to a platform in London to lecture, in her strong Austrian accent and with her rapid delivery, to an audience of 3,000 people, the opening gambit of a lecture tour covering the world. Her heart is in its wild places, her companions its creatures, but in their interests she has braved the rigours of publicity which can wrack the nerves more severely than charging rhinos or stampeding elephants.

So she became world-famous, and this story of her life, from its happy beginnings as one of a large, close-knit family in the feudal and artistic society of Austria before the First World War, to her retreat among the animals on the shores of Lake Naivasha in Kenya, needs no introduction from me or anyone else. It is a unique story, told with the directness and simplicity of all her writings: the story of a generous, creative and artistic person, with a great fund of affection for her fellow creatures, who has devoted her life to observing them as individuals in order to discover how they think, feel and behave, to recording the results with brush and pen, and to pleading their cause in the world at large. But this book is not a treatise, or in any sense a polemic. It is an adventure tale, the personal story of a woman of courage, gaiety and zest for life. 'A day in the bush is never dull,' she remarks. Nor is a page in her autobiography.

ELSPETH HUXLEY

I

The St. Bernard
in the Bus

Was it a portent that as children our favourite game was a lion hunt and that because of my blonde hair and reputation for being a quick runner, I was always assigned the role of the lioness? During the summer holidays there were often fifteen of us children staying at the Seifenmühle, our estate in Austria, enough to provide plenty of hunters for two lions. The part of the male lion was always allotted to my favourite cousin, Peter. Since the estate was very large it sometimes took the hunters several hours to locate their quarry and occasionally they failed to do so within the prescribed time limit. In that case the hunt was over and we lions had won.

It was an exciting game; if we saw the pursuers closing in on one of our dens the other lion would roar to distract their attention and then run for dear life.

All my happiest childhood memories are attached to Seifen-mühle, which belonged to my mother's family, the Weisshuhns. They were paper manufacturers who owned a number of factories and mills. Amongst other activities, they recycled bank notes and I well remember the time, after the First World War, when one needed a trillion note to buy a dozen eggs. Since paper, however, was still valuable, the bank notes were stored in gigantic silos which stood in the yards of our factories. In these we children made tunnels and played amongst the billions and trillions – a strange introduction to money, but perhaps it helped me to realise how worthless it can become when man-made values change.

As many as thirty people were sometimes staying at the Villa Friederike in the holidays and Weisshuhn cousins came not only from Austria but from Germany, Italy, England and America. Friends came too and the inscription on a door at the entrance of the villa was typical of our family:

> Ten were invited, twenty have come,
> Put water in the soup and make them welcome.

The place was a paradise for children. There was a tennis court and a swimming pool. Our ambition was to race a bicycle from the high diving board down a wooden rail into the water without turning over, or to sit in a little four-wheel wagon and roll at great speed into the pool, trying not to sink when we landed in the water. We and our cousins conducted our private Olympic Games; we competed in throwing the discus, in high jumps, in target shooting and riding and in obstacle races. For the birthdays of the grown-ups we put on plays and on many evenings we gave concerts at which we sang *Lieder*, or our improvised orchestra played.

The highlight of each summer was the Harvest Festival. As soon as the last load of ripe corn had been stored in the barns, the peasants arrived, sitting in beautifully decorated wagons and wearing home-made fancy dresses. The manager presented Uncle Karl, the head of the family, with a crown six feet high made of corn, poppies, daisies and cornflowers. Then a small girl in a white dress, brittle with starch, her hair brushed tightly back, her face shining, stammered a poem. Afterwards we children carried trays of cakes, sweets, fruit juices and schnaps to the peasants and then the real fun began.

We all piled onto the harvest wagon and drove to the barn which, with highly coloured flags and ribbons dangling all around, had been transformed into a dance hall. To the sound of a concertina and two fiddles Uncle Karl opened the ball with the manager's wife, while her husband danced with my aunt, after which we all joined in.

Among the people on the estate I remember especially our coachman, Orga, a Hungarian with a stiff leg and many black-haired children. He often took me into the forest to collect mushrooms; I was very fond of him.

Hunting was a tradition in our family and there were plenty of roebucks, hares, foxes and partridges on the estate. I always hated the organised shoots in which the guns were placed in a wide circle, waiting for the beaters to drive the terrified hare to its end. But, in general, at that age I took shoots in my stride. The only evidence of my distaste was that I did not like eating game and I absolutely refused to eat hare, with the result that I got punished for my fussiness.

It was when I was fifteen that I had a curious experience which made a lasting impression on me. I was walking with our game-keeper on his afternoon round. We had seen a fair number of deer before we sat down to rest on the edge of a forest glade. Soon a roebuck appeared and made his way to the side of a little brook, nibbling as he went. The light was waning and the stillness of the forest seemed to enhance the beauty of the animal as it moved towards us. I remember that I was actually reflecting on the senselessness of shooting such a perfect creature when the keeper handed me his rifle, telling me to shoot the roebuck because its antlers were malformed. I aimed, shot and killed. What had I done? How could I think so lovingly of the deer and a moment later kill it? Would I ever be able to trust myself again? Then, before we slung the buck on a pole the keeper proudly presented me with a twig of pine dipped in the animal's blood. At dinner the twig was still in my buttonhole and my uncle, who was a keen sportsman, congratulated me on getting my first buck but I felt like a murderess and vowed never again to shoot for sport.

There were other incidents too that burned deep into my subconscious and were released much later when I determined to devote my life to saving wild animals.

There was the marten that our manager kept in a wire cage so tiny that he could hardly turn round in it. He was there to amuse us children.

There were the small fox cubs which we picked out of a hessian bag and were allowed to keep as pets but for only a short period, after which they disappeared and were used to train terriers to drive foxes out of their dens.

Above all, there was my albino rabbit, Hasi, whom I loved. Then one day, it was during the war, we had rabbit stew. When I remarked to my mother how good it was, she replied unconcernedly that it was Hasi.

All these incidents seemed to have been distilled in a dream I had years later, in 1940, while I was camping with Mary Leakey, the wife of the famous anthropologist Dr Louis Leakey. We were excavating remains of early man in the Ngorongoro crater in Tanganyika – now Tanzania (this was long before the area was made a National Park). The crater was teeming with wild animals but in spite of our paradise-like surroundings, the setting of my dream was in Vienna, early on a grey, drizzling November morning.

A man was standing in a long, deserted street waiting for a bus to take him to work. He was the only living creature among the grey walls of the houses, with the exception of a St. Bernard dog who seemed equally lonely. After some time the dog walked up to the man and, rubbing his head against his legs, offered his affection and companionship. The man was touched by his friendliness and scratched his silky coat in response. When he boarded the bus the dog followed his new master automatically. Both received a warm welcome amongst the passengers who, travelling each morning together to work, found the presence of this dog a welcome change. They made a great fuss of him, to which he responded by placing his big head on their knees but, as is the habit of a St. Bernard, he left traces of saliva on their clothes. This soon provoked complaints and finally protests, and the man was asked to take the dog away. Although he had certainly felt proud when earlier much attention had been paid to him because of the dog, he now pushed him off the bus into the street. By then the drizzling rain had turned to snow which continued to fall all day long. When in the late afternoon the man was returning home, he passed the spot where he had pushed the dog off the bus. There he saw a mound covered with freshly fallen snow.

*

Of the inhabitants of Seifenmühle the most colourful personality was my great-grandfather, a giant of a man who was charming. He also had a big heart but his poor wife put up with his adventures and their marriage remained as solid as a rock; indeed, it was the rock on which the couple's children, grandchildren and great-grandchildren were securely based. It was he, my maternal great-grandfather, who introduced the first car into the district. It was bright red and to the peasants it seemed to be a smoke-spitting devil. To stop the advance of this terrifying monster they sprinkled cut glass on the road. Great-grandfather's reply was to throw little bags of peppermints to the children whenever he passed through a village. This gave them a better impression of the monster and so well established did the custom become that even in our days, when cars were common, it continued.

My great-grandfather owned amongst his many factories one sited on the river Mohra and here he determined to set up the first water turbine in the country. To do this he had a tunnel cut through a hill and diverted the course of the river into it. He was sure that the drop of about a thousand feet at the mouth of the tunnel would generate sufficient power to electrify the paper factories in the area. The expense involved in cutting the tunnel was considerable so great-grandfather asked his bankers for a loan. At first they were reluctant to underwrite such a bold project but in the end they consented.

The day on which the flood waters were to be released through the tunnel was one of great anxiety for our family. The Government, and financial and technical authorities had sent representatives to see the water roar out but when the long-awaited moment came nothing happened. Nor on the second or the third day was there any sign of water; great-grandfather was faced with disaster. Then on the fourth day a trickle appeared, which soon swelled to a mighty flood; the new epoch of water power had begun. The failure of the headwaves to come on the first three days was probably due to the dryness of the surface of the tunnel, which had to be saturated with moisture before water could pass through it.

Great-grandfather's next project was to build a dam in a narrow valley of Seifenmühle, which was flanked by precipitous cliffs. He believed that it would power a reservoir which would service all the surrounding country. But this project was far too daring for his contemporaries and it was not until after the Second World War that the biggest dam, in what was no longer Austria but Czechoslovakia, was set up in that valley of Seifenmühle.

When he made his plans great-grandfather foresaw that the Villa Friederike might one day be drowned if his dam came into operation. He took precautions against this calamity. The villa was designed after a prefabricated building in the United States; it could be dismantled and set up on higher ground.

The United States always attracted great-grandfather, he went there six times with his sons. On one of these occasions Edison offered him a partnership. He would have accepted but for his wife's reluctance to see him invest all his capital in risky experiments – after all, he had twelve children to educate.

Despite his many activities, great-grandfather took a deep interest in his large family. One of his habits was to drop a gold coin into the first bath taken by each new baby; he believed that it would bring them good luck. I vividly remember how angry he was when he arrived too late for my young sister's bath and found her already dressed. From each of his trips abroad he returned with a present for every grand- and great-grandchild, although there were thirty of us. I can still recall many little incidents connected with him; for instance, once when we were taking a walk together we passed a larch tree that was covered with small growths, the symptom of some parasitical disease. Great-grandfather began at once to pluck them and asked me to help him, stressing that when one saw that there was a job to be done, one should act immediately since the opportunity might not recur. I have often recalled his words.

One morning when he was eighty-two he drove in a sleigh, with a keeper to inspect the forest. As they came to a steep hill the sleigh turned over and rolled down the slope. Great-grandfather was not injured but seemed shaken. Nevertheless, he insisted that they should go on and look at the forest.

During lunch he complained of a slight headache and afterwards went upstairs to take a rest. Half an hour later, someone entered his bedroom and found him dead.

We children watched his funeral from a window. The procession, headed by the local fire brigade band, seemed never-ending. It consisted of the peasants from the estates, the factory staff, great-grandfather's many friends and most of the inhabitants of the local town. How little did any of us then realise that within a generation our strongly-knit family would be scattered all over the world, with little left in common except our deep roots in Seifenmühle.

My father, Ober Baurat Victor Gessner, was a civil servant, and later, during the First World War, a Colonel in charge of a motorised unit. Although I loved and respected him, I was rather frightened of him. He frequently told us stories, made us observe the habits of ants and other little creatures, and was sometimes very affectionate. But on other occasions, and without the slightest warning, he would ignore us, tease us or punish us in a somewhat sadistic way.

I felt much closer to my mother, who was attractive, gifted and charming. I was very proud of her, indeed she was something of a goddess to me. She had a lovely soprano voice, painted well and was the centre of every party. The only complaint I had against her was that far too often we were left in the care of our nanny and later, in that of our governess. As a result, though I adored my mother, our cook, Milli, was my closest friend and the person I went to for sympathy and comfort. She had endless patience and was a willing audience when, dressed in my mother's shawls, I danced or acted under my 'stage name' of Bobrika Jenjar.

I worshipped my mother and could not understand why sometimes she let me down, as when she forgot a promise to take me out or discussed with her friends a poem I had been too shy to give her and had hidden under her pillow.

Besides my parents there was my sister Traute, a year older than I, and also my sister Dorle who was nine years younger.

It is not for me to say what I was like as a child but I can quote from a letter my mother wrote me on my sixtieth birthday. She confessed that when I was born on 20 January 1910, I was a great disappointment as my parents had been hoping for a boy. I was christened Friederike, the name given to every second daughter in my mother's family. To this was added Victoria, apparently the hope was that I would be a peace-loving champion. My father, unable to reconcile himself to the fact that I was a girl, called me Fritz, treated me as if I were a son and encouraged me to wear boy's clothes.

According to my mother I was not afraid of anything, except a mythical personage called 'Bubutz', whom Milli had invented to keep me in order. I had, it seems, a passion for flowers, in particular for violets and every effort was made to give me a plant for my birthday, since in my eyes no other present could compare with it. I loved music and could sight-read before I knew my alphabet; if I were hurt I would ask for some Chopin to be played to relieve my pain. In our family it was natural to be musical for everyone sang or played some instrument and even the servants sang Slavonic folk songs in counterpoint.

At school I learned quickly and apparently I was so conscientious about my homework that I would even ask to leave a party to finish it in time for next day's class.

What I myself remember best was how Peter and I would slip out of the Villa Friederike after dinner and lie in a meadow, looking at the stars and discussing what we would do when we were grown-up. For both of us this meant exploring various countries and discovering new animals. In a way our dreams have come true for Peter has settled in Alberta, Canada and for the last forty years I have lived in Kenya.

Villa Friederike, Seifenmühle

Celebrating Christmas. Joy (on the right)
with her parents and sister Traute

With great-grandmama
on the way to collect
mushrooms. Joy on donkey,
mama and Traute
in background

Joy as 'Geisha' in
a play written by the
children to celebrate the
birthday of a relation

Traute and Joy (on the left)

My first – and only – roebuck

Oma

2

First Love

At the end of the First World War our homeland ceased to be
Austrian Silesia – and became Czechoslovakia. We had always
spoken German but now Czech, which none of us knew, was to
be our language. There was an occasion when Uncle Karl had to
address a government delegation who were visiting one of our
factories. He started off with the few words of Czech he had
learned but soon hesitated and, with a charming smile, continued
in German, to the applause of all those present.

Some of our properties and factories were confiscated because
all had been registered under the name of the firm and together
they totalled more than it was permitted for any one company
or individual, to own. Millions of people had been uprooted by
the war and could not adapt themselves to a new way of life.
On the other hand, certain people had grown rich and powerful.

I was still quite small when I became aware that my mother's
family, the Weisshuhns, seemed to be considered grander than my
father's family, the Gessners. This certainly became apparent
when the Weisshuhn cousins had whipped cream on their
Torten, whereas we had only beaten-up white of egg and I grew
painfully conscious of the disparity when these cousins laughed
at me for having nails in the soles of my shoes to make them last
longer – something they had no need to consider. Above all I was
embarrassed when Peter asked me if I would not rather be a
Weisshuhn like him.

I felt that this uncomfortable situation must hurt my parents
and would have liked to protect them but they were already on

rather strained terms.

I believe it was to rescue their marriage that when I was eight, hoping for a boy, they decided to have another child. In the event, a third daughter, Dorle, was born. Four years later my parents divorced.

My mother then moved to Vienna and very soon remarried. My sisters and I did not like our stepfather so for a short time we all stayed with our own father. Several governesses were engaged to look after us but eventually it was decided that Traute and I should live in Vienna with our maternal grandmother. Only Dorle remained with our father. From that time onwards we saw her rarely and lost touch with the Gessners.

I spent the next four years at a boarding school that was run on new and indeed, unique teaching methods. It was one of six for children between the ages of twelve and eighteen (three for boys and three for girls), established after the war by the Austrian Government.

We had Swedish gym classes, played a lot of games and, when weather permitted, we did our lessons in the gardens. One innovation was that teaching was chiefly by question and answer and by acting various historical scenes. Our teachers were drawn from all over the world and geography was taught by films, accompanied by lectures given by inhabitants of the various countries we were being shown.

My particular school had been a Military Academy; it had large gardens and playing fields, an indoor riding school, a swimming pool, a sick bay and a chapel. There were laboratories where we made up various concoctions which I always feared might explode; much more to my liking, there were many rooms, elegantly decorated in stucco and gilt, where we could practise our music and a large dining room which was often converted into a concert hall, where we gave performances of such works as 'Eine kleine Nachtmusik' or Haydn's 'Toy Symphony'. I was lucky to have piano lessons from a professor who had previously taught at the Mozarteum in Salzburg. I tried also to play the violin but soon found that my hands were too small.

We put on French and English plays, we modelled, we made linocuts and we painted. Painting was what I liked most, and

I specially enjoyed decorating the walls of our living quarters with murals; once I was asked to paint a village band playing at a Harvest Festival. At the time I hero-worshipped Toni Konrad, the conductor of the Vienna Symphony Orchestra and brother of our headmaster. In my mural I portrayed him as the conductor of the village band. The likeness turned out to be striking and one day Konrad came to look at his portrait. This was more than I had hoped for, and when afterwards we were introduced it was the high spot of my term.

Entry into these experimental schools was based on competition and therefore, on merit, so the children were drawn from all social classes, which helped to break down prejudices and taught me to respect individual achievement.

Although I liked the school, I left it when I was fifteen to concentrate on music and from then on lived with my maternal grandmother.

We called her Oma. It is to her I owe anything that may be good in me. She showed endless patience in trying to understand my problems and helped me by example, rather than by advice, in coping with my difficulties. She told me that since she would not always be there to protect me, I would in the long run be responsible for my decisions. To prepare me, she left me free and trusted me completely. As a result, I never did anything behind her back and always talked over my problems with her.

Oma was not daunted by growing old; at seventy she took painting lessons, she played the piano and sang in a rich alto voice, and she practised daily to improve her technique – it never occurred to her that age might put a limit to her learning. Oma's warm nature attracted people like a magnet and consequently her house was always full of guests, whom she reassured and comforted as she did her own family.

During the next two years I worked for the State Piano Certificate which qualified one to teach. Its schedule was less rigid than that of the Academy of Music but it also required the study of counterpoint, harmony, composition and the history of music. I worked hard, too hard, for I strained both my hands. They proved to be not large enough to give me any hope of making a career as a professional pianist. I managed quite well

so long as there were not a lot of octaves in succession, but when
I saw the programme set for the examination my heart sank.
The scales and the classic composition I could cope with but the
last piece was by a modern composer, and in it there were
endless successions of octaves. However hard I tried to practise
this passage I always ended up with cramp in both my hands.
On the morning of the examination I had an accident; I was
slicing some hard, Danish pumpernickel when the knife slipped
and cut a deep gash in the tip of my left thumb. If I didn't appear
on that day it meant postponing the examination for a whole year,
so I bandaged the wound as tightly as I could and hoped for the
best. The examiner saw my bandage, he was sympathetic and
seemed pleased with the way I thundered out my scales and played
Bach and Beethoven. When it came to the virtuoso piece, by
extraordinary good luck, the bandage tore and blood spilled all
over the keys. The examiner stopped me at once and since I
had satisfied him with what he had already heard, he let me pass
the test with flying colours. I had not expected this, I was only
seventeen, a year younger than students are normally allowed
to qualify as teachers, and I was overjoyed.

But, what was I to do next? I realised that I could never become
a concert pianist and I did not want to teach. Renouncing a musical career I took a two-year course in dress-making and acquired
the Gremium Diploma. Whilst doing this I spent my evenings
drawing from life, learning how to restore pictures and taking
singing lessons. I also learned typing and shorthand and had a
go at designing posters and book jackets. I was certainly busy
enough but I could not decide on any career.

In the summer holidays we went to Seifenmühle where, despite
my love for the place, whole days spent on the tennis court or in
the swimming pool bored me to distraction. I therefore asked
Oma if I could take lessons with a sculptor called Kapps, who
lived not far from Seifenmühle and who had recently made a
marble sarcophagus for our family vault. At the moment he was
working on a gigantic figure of Christ which was to be a war
memorial. It was made in copper. I watched, fascinated, as he
worked on the different sections of the body and then joined the
various metal sheets together. I had never seen this method of

young cousin of theirs; he had come to Austria from the Argentine to see his father who was very ill. Oma invited him to tea. He came but gave no sign of being particularly interested in Traute. Soon afterwards his father died and he returned to the Argentine. Our amazement was quite considerable when he wrote from the boat asking Traute to follow him to Buenos Aires, where he was working as an engineer, and on arrival to become his wife. She was thrilled and accepted, apparently without hesitation. I was puzzled, for I believed that marriage should be based on love and on a close identity of values between the two people concerned. Yet in Traute's case I saw no sign of any deep feelings for this 'instant' fiancé, only delight at his unusual form of proposal and a great sense of excitement and romance at the prospect of going to South America. Traute was in fact as unprepared for marriage as I was and years later she told me that it was the ship's doctor who had enlightened her on what sexual relationships implied. The marriage was not a happy one. After the birth of their only child, the couple returned to Austria where they divorced. Traute did not marry again.

Though she and I had very different temperaments, I felt lonely when she left us so I was delighted when Uncle Karl telephoned from Troppau to ask me to join him and his actress friend on a trip to Italy. For as long as I could remember Uncle Karl had been unhappy with his wife and he had everyone's sympathy when he indulged in the various escapades which his warm-hearted nature seemed to demand.

Oma and I had often met this actress and fully understood Uncle Karl's devotion to her. I was therefore allowed to accept the invitation to 'act as chaperone'. It proved to be a very happy time for all of us. This was my first visit to Switzerland, Uncle Karl generously lent me his car so I was able to go exploring in all directions. I got to know the Engadin well; I walked up to the hut where Segantini had painted; I reached the glacier which inspired Nietzsche to write *Also sprach Zarathustra;* I climbed to the source of the river Inn. I also drove to the Italian Lakes and to the Dolomites and spent many hours in the galleries of Venice and Milan. To make it all the more pleasant, behind all this sightseeing was the knowledge that by my presence, or rather by my tactful absences, I was enabling two people to be very happy.

In our large family there were several unsatisfactory marriages and so from childhood I had learned to accept what might be called 'long leash' relationships, provided they were conducted with tact and did not hurt anyone.

During this trip I became quite fond of Uncle Karl's friend and when, on my return to Vienna, I had thoughts about a stage career she arranged a meeting between her agent and myself. It took place at the Café Sacher. I came into an elegant, crowded room, feeling rather nervous. There I was greeted by an elderly hunchback who licked his thumb and wiped it along my eyebrows. I stiffened in embarrassment, whereupon he laughed and said he only wanted to know whether they were natural or touched up. He then suggested that we should move to a private room. To this I gladly agreed, fearing that if not I might be in for more public eyebrow licking.

It was a cold, rainy, November day which made the red room look all the cosier. The little man told me that he wished to test my acting technique, and that for this I must play the part of a jealous wife who wanted to win her husband back from his mistress. I was told to leave the room and that when I re-entered it I would find him playing the role of the errant husband. I went out and waited until he called me. I discovered that he had switched off all the lights except for one near the couch on which he had settled himself. I moved slowly towards him, trying to control my amusement at this far from seductive scene. Unfortunately, I noticed the unmistakable glee in the man's little eyes as he tried to play the part of the *roué* – so I burst out laughing and this put an end to any prospect I had of going on the stage.

Strangely enough, not long afterwards my riding master asked me if I would like to ride a white stallion in a performance of Max Reinhardt's *The Miracle*. This was going to take place in a vast arena in Vienna and the riding school had been invited to provide a girl, with a good seat on a horse, who would be capable of controlling a stallion. I thought this might be great fun but when I discussed the plan with Oma she refused to allow me to take the part.

My next venture was to ask a professional photographer, who made exquisite colour photographs, just like miniatures, if he would take me on as a pupil. Fearing that he might train up a rival, he had so far refused to teach anyone but I succeeded in convincing him that I had no intention of becoming a competitor – and he agreed to take me on. In his studio I learned to note minute details, which later helped me in my flower paintings, but I did not find this type of art very satisfying.

It was about this time that my relationship with my mother reached crisis point. We sisters never raised the subject of my father but I felt I wanted to defend him when my mother criticised him. As for my stepfather, whom she persistently tried to make us accept, I was jealous of him and at times positively hated him for taking our mother away from us. For some time I had been going to see my mother only when I knew that her husband was out. I had loved these visits, during which we played music and sketched together. They were the only occasions when I had my mother to myself. But she now used them to praise her new husband at the expense of my father and so in the end I stopped going to see her.

I very rarely saw my father for after he remarried he built himself a villa at Troppau, but when I did see him, he was always kind and interested in what I was doing and he never tried to interfere in my life, or find fault with me. We wrote to each other occasionally.

One morning, when I was working in the photographer's studio, my mother rang me up. She had never done such a thing before and I felt frightened. In a cool, detached, totally insensitive voice she announced that she had just heard that my father had died. He had been ill lately but I had not thought that he was in immediate danger. My mother further informed me that a post mortem had revealed that he had died of an unknown disease of the spleen and that in consequence this organ of his was now exhibited in the Prague Medical Museum. I just managed to replace the receiver before I collapsed.

Oma did her best to prevent a complete break between my

mother and myself and was particularly affectionate and understanding to me at this time. I remember especially a Christmas
Eve when I had refused to go to my mother's home, where I
knew I should find her new husband. Oma came into my room,
hugged me and gave me her most treasured jewel. This was a
cameo brooch with an exquisite carving of the goddess Diana
wearing the Order of the Golden Fleece. The cameo was set in
gold and diamonds and had a fascinating history.

It had been given to Baron von Sedlnitzky, the Chief of
Police, by the Emperor Franz Joseph. Oma knew the Baron's
grand-daughter who had inherited it and after her death bought
it. It is rare among cameos because it shows the full figure of
the goddess. It is also of exceptional interest in that it was given
to Baron von Sedlnitzky in lieu of the Order of the Golden Fleece,
which could only be awarded to great aristocrats. The Order of
the Golden Fleece was founded in 1429 by Philip the Good, Duke
of Burgundy. It was the highest European Order of Chivalry.
Later it was in the gift of the Habsburgs, both Spanish and
Austrian. After the First World War and the fall of the Habsburgs
the Austrian branch of the order was abolished; in 1930 the
Spanish branch came to an end.

When Oma pinned it on me to console me for this sad Christmas, she said, 'I wish that you may always be happy when you
wear it.' I treasured the cameo till the day, thirty-five years later,
when it was stolen.

We knew a good many painters and so I sat several times for
my portrait. I still possess a charcoal sketch by Walter Klier,
which I liked the best of all. Henri de Bouvard painted a full
length oil of me, which was pleasing, if a little conventional.
Another painter friend produced the head of a girl with dark
brown eyes, amber coloured hair and a narrow face. As a painting
it was striking, but knowing that I have blue eyes, blonde hair
and a round face I was astonished when he told me that he saw
me like that. I have never understood what attracts people to
modern art, whether that of the Impressionists, the Futurists, or
abstract painters.

At one of the previews at the Sezession, Vienna's leading gallery of contemporary art, I was given a ticket to the *Gschnas*, the famous fancy-dress ball of the art world. Though I had not enjoyed the Hofburg Ball, I was very keen to go to this one, which was the high point of the Vienna carnival. With the help of a talented art student, my white satin Hofburg gown was transformed into a fancy dress in which half of the white satin was painted and so was part of my body. It was certainly very original and with Oma's reluctant blessing I set off for the Künstlerhaus, where the familiar rooms had been transformed by daring murals into the most alluring scene. I was both fascinated and scared and my first reaction was to have a quick look round and then bolt for home, but before I had been able to make my way out of the picturesque crowd my shoulders were grabbed by a masked apache. With the words, 'You are mine' he carried me away. Thus I was swept into my first love affair. It aroused emotions sometimes almost beyond what I could bear. When, after two years, it ended I was left with a little dachshund called Plinkus and a deep wound in my heart, which took a long time to heal.

At this time psycho-analysis was very fashionable in Vienna, where it had originated. Caught up in the general enthusiasm, I began to watch all the people I met to see if they behaved according to the theories I had been reading about and I interpreted their actions as manifestations of their subconscious. Having been warned by friends that I would only be able to appreciate the benefits of the new science if I were myself prepared to be analysed, I duly spent an hour every day relaxing on the couch of a famous psycho-analyst. There, at his request, I talked about everything that came into my mind. It was believed that in doing this one would unknowingly reveal reactions which had been suppressed at the time and had thereby damaged what should have been one's normal responses. I tried to let my thoughts pour out at random but the psycho-analyst kept interrupting, asking me to concentrate on my childhood.

I found this very unsatisfactory so I went to another analyst but after more than a year, having derived no benefit – except that of obtaining a patient listener to my problems – I stopped the treatment. As far as I could judge the only advice I had been given was to get married. However this course of analysis did do one thing for me: it made me aware of the danger of attributing deep significance to the most natural reactions. It also convinced me that the high figure of suicides in Austria might well be due to the vogue for analysis. During this period I myself narrowly escaped such a fate.

While I was undergoing analysis I was also attending lectures on psychiatry at the medical faculty. Learning about cases of extreme mental illness made me understand something of the tragedy of the human race, but probing into these abnormalities frightened me, so, looking for something healthier to give a purpose to my life I returned to sculpture.

Oma, who was aware of my growing distress, encouraged me to have lessons from the distinguished sculptor, Prof. Wilhelm Frass. His studio was in the Prater, the woody park which stretches along the Danube and which had been at one time the Imperial hunting forest. A small part of the Prater, near Vienna, was used on occasion for international exhibitions. When, in 1873, Austria held a world exhibition, two large buildings resembling Greek temples were built there. They faced each other. Later they were converted into studios for artists engaged on very large works.

It was on a lovely spring day that, after walking through the woods, I reached the two Greek temples, stopped by a fountain, went up the broad flagged stairs that led to the portico and knocked on a studio door.

Frass welcomed me. He was wearing a white overall and a white cap covered his white hair. Smiling he said: 'What a nice surprise that it should be you who wishes to become my pupil, because since I saw you at an art exhibition I have wanted to do a bust of you.' From this moment we became great friends and my friendship soon extended to the sculptor's family. With his wife and two sons I spent many happy evenings playing chamber music.

What I most admired about Frass was the way in which he handled everything himself – from the design to the completed work. Very few sculptors do this.

He taught me the importance of designing a figure so that it satisfied the demands of the medium in which it was going to be executed – obviously stone, marble, bronze, wax and wood make different demands. To me, releasing a figure from a block of wood or stone seemed much more exciting than building up a figure from clay. For this reason, I returned to wood carving and made several nude figures. In one I was able to express my reaction to death.

I had always been very frightened of death and I had succeeded till then in never seeing a dead person. I was therefore terribly shocked when a drunken man ran in front of a car in which I was a passenger: at one moment he was running, at the next he was immobile – dead. The incident haunted me for days. I could not forget his legs stretched out stiffly across the road, mercifully a crowd of people hid the rest of his body from me. I could not get this scene out of my mind and when walking to the studio I looked at the straight boles of the trees, they seemed to me to be the dead man's legs.

Then, one day I saw them not as the legs of a corpse but as the legs of a girl who was standing upright, turning her head aside and hiding her head with her arms. I modelled this figure in clay and as I did so I felt strangely calm. It was as though my fear of death had been transferred to the statue. As I looked at it, the figure appeared to reveal all my emotional distress and I think it must have communicated something of the sort to other people, for Frass was impressed by it and suggested that I should carve it in wood.

At one time I became interested in Indonesian carving and I thought of going to Bali and asked the advice of Walter Spiess who lived there. He was a White Russian, a painter and a musician. In his reply he wrote that I would either have to have a private income, or marry a Dutch planter. Since I did not have the means to live there without working and I had no wish to marry a Dutch planter, I dropped the plan. Instead I thought of joining a man who was proposing to explore the Solomon Islands which had always interested me because of the islanders' carvings. However, when the explorer suggested that if I went with him he would leave his wife with the mutual friend who had introduced us, and that I should become his mistress, I gave up this plan too.

Of course I would have liked to marry, but the men I attracted were not of the type I wished to spend my life with, or would have liked to have as the father of my children. In the circumstances I spent a lot of time alone, taking long walks in the forests, or skiing, getting as near to nature and as far away from the social round as I could.

Suddenly, a new interest came into my life. I had friends amongst the medical students and they arranged that I should secretly join them in the dissecting room. They warned me that I might well faint but I was far too absorbed in the coordination of bones, tendons and tissues to have any physical reaction. Indeed, I became so interested that I decided I would give up sculpting for medicine. This meant that I would need to spend two years studying for the Matriculation examination which would allow me to enter the university; at the same time, I would need to brush up my Latin. Poor Oma, it is only now writing about this time that I realise how well she understood me and how deeply she loved me. I was twenty-three, most of my cousins and girl-friends had either married, or got jobs, and here was I determined to start going to school again for seven years – as far as ever from settling down and a heavy financial burden to her.

My new studies did not come easily to me. I had never been good at mathematics, chemistry or physics and in this post-graduate course I had no access to laboratories; as a result I got bored and often depressed. It was difficult, too, working with juniors and then there were the many hours of homework which did not allow me much time for meeting interesting scientists and artists or for my skiing weekends, which I loved.

It was on one of these that I met Victor von Klarwill, known to his friends as Ziebel and considered by them to be one of Vienna's eccentrics. He told me of his great interest in birds, of his love for nature, of his wish to get away from sophisticated city life, and how in his endeavours to escape he had corresponded with Alain Gerbault, who had now settled in the Marquesas Islands. Ziebel had thought of joining him but Gerbault had indicated that he would prefer to keep the Islands to himself.

We saw each other every day but I was very much surprised when, after three weeks, Ziebel proposed, and suggested that we should get married at once. He begged me to cut short my studies, assuring me that he trusted I would never need to earn my living and promised that together we would look for and find a home which would fulfil all our dreams. We were married in the spring of 1935.

Ziebel was a successful businessman with a large circle of friends, and a passion for skiing. During the summers we travelled widely and in the winters we skied. My husband spoiled me and did his best to make my life as easy as possible, but in doing so he unknowingly made it more difficult.

We had seen too little of each other before our marriage for me to realise how different our views on life were. I tried to share his beliefs and to understand his behaviour but both were strange to me and, as a result, cast a shadow over our marriage. I also found the purely social life I was now leading extremely frustrating and I only bore it because I knew it was temporary, and that in time we would find a place where we could live life as we wanted it to be.

Already we had contacted the Governor of Tahiti and been in touch with people in Tasmania and California, but without success. Now we were in correspondence with a Swiss farmer living in Kenya. Because Ziebel did not want to burn his boats in Vienna before he knew whether I would like Africa, he suggested that I should go out alone and stay with the farmer's family and have a look at the country. Since he did not wish people to know that we were thinking of leaving Austria for good, he wanted me to keep my journey secret.

On our drive to Genoa, where I was boarding the boat, we stopped in Carinthia with some friends. We found them discussing the remarkable gifts of a local fortune-teller. I was very sceptical about such people but this man certainly seemed to have made some impressive and inexplicable forecasts. So I thought it would be fun to try him out. I scribbled down two questions: one – was I going to continue to live where I was at present? and two – would I have children? I did not sign the paper, or give my address but placed it in a sealed envelope and asked my friends to keep the reply until I called for it.

In Genoa Ziebel and I parted. I had never before left Europe and travelling alone frightened me but he comforted me with his love and his conviction that all would turn out for the best for both of us.

When we sailed I stood on deck and watched him getting smaller and smaller, till he finally disappeared in the haze of the coastline. It was 12 May, 1937, the day of George VI's coronation.

Summer, 1931

Terracotta by
Prof. Wilhelm Frass,
Vienna, 1931

At the Lido

Skiing with Ziebel
(Victor) von Klarwill

By boat to Kenya, 1937

Peter Bally

3

Introduction
to Africa

It was at dawn next day that I had my first sight of Africa; and not long afterwards we reached Port Said. I rushed to the top deck and saw the Sudanese porters running up the gangway looking, with their muscular bodies and fuzzy hairstyles, as though they had stepped out of an Egyptian frieze.

I was fascinated by the incandescent light, the strange smell of the harbour, the white, flat-roofed buildings, the floating, brightly coloured robes of the people. In all the many parts of Europe I had visited, I had never seen anything like this and yet I felt curiously at home.

When we were told that the boat would take two days to go through the Suez Canal I decided to join some passengers who were going to Cairo and would rejoin the ship at Port Sudan. We visited the bazaar, sipped coffee out of tiny porcelain cups and ate dates. Only half an hour was allowed for the visit to the museum to see the Tutankhamun excavations, then the rest of the party rushed off to a big lunch at Shepheards Hotel. I was so overwhelmed by what I had glimpsed that I skipped the lunch and stayed on at the museum to have more time to study these amazing exhibits.

Afterwards, when we were riding on camels round the Gizeh Pyramids, the agent who conducted our tour came to tell us that our boat had passed much more quickly than was expected through the Suez Canal, so we had no time to visit the remaining

sites and must now get into a taxi and rush through the desert to
board the ship. But when we reached Port Sudan after dark there
was no sign of our boat. We spent a most uncomfortable night
in the only hotel at Port Sudan and next morning, as the ship had
still not arrived, we hired a glass-bottomed boat and I discovered
a new world of infinite beauty. Gliding slowly above coral of all
shades were unbelievably beautiful fish – some swimming in large
schools among tunnels and crevices, other darting singly between
bright seaweeds. These fish were of incredible shapes, their
iridescent colours glittering in the subdued light of the under-
water world.

Unknowingly, I had learned a lesson which was to be typical
of my African experience: I had gone out in pursuit of something
I never found but instead came upon a treasure much greater
than I had ever hoped to discover.

When at last our boat arrived, I observed several new passengers; they had come on board at Cairo. Among them was a man
who aroused a strange feeling in me – I felt as though I had known
him all my life.

Next morning he asked me to be his partner at deck tennis
and introduced himself as Peter Bally, a Swiss. Later, we had
drinks together and as we talked I had a strong impression that
we belonged to each other. During the following days I learned
of Peter's interest in botany and of the research he had done in
India into the medicinal properties of herbs. Recently he had been
in Israel where he had discussed with Dr Chaim Weizmann the
possibility of cultivating such plants in an effort to revive herbal
medicine, which has fewer disastrous side effects than many of
the synthetic drugs in use today. Peter showed me a book he had
written on that subject which had recently been published in
Switzerland and told me that he proposed to continue his studies
in South Africa. But before this he was to stay in Kenya to study
the botanical collection in the Nairobi Museum, and also to have
a car equipped which he had designed for his further travels. It
was entirely self-contained, a complete home on wheels.

By the time we reached Mombasa, we had grown close and
Peter told me about his unhappy marriage which was being
dissolved. We now parted, he to stay in Nairobi and I to visit the

Swiss farmer's family.

I was torn between my feeling for Peter and my knowledge that Ziebel loved me and trusted me to find a home for us in Kenya. For some weeks the conflict continued but when Peter arrived unexpectedly to visit me, before we could even say a word we fell into each other's arms.

After this I knew there was only one thing for me to do: I must return at once to Vienna and discuss the situation with Ziebel. When I got there I learnt that from my letters he had guessed that something was wrong, but when I told him about the situation between Peter and myself he was crushed.

Hoping to give our marriage another chance, I arranged to stay with friends in Zurich. I wanted to be busy and I succeeded in persuading Dr Vogt, the Director of the Zurich Museum of Natural History, to allow me to join students who were excavating the Lindenhof. This stood on a hill in the centre of the city; in mediaeval times a fort had been built upon it, below which were the remains of a much older fortification. Dr Vogt was, at first, doubtful about my ability to stand up to the very rough conditions in which the students were working, but soon he saw that I could do this and we became great friends. Despite my genuine efforts to improve matters between Ziebel and myself, they only got worse. In the end, he behaved most generously and made our divorce as easy as possible. We parted friends and I am glad that, several years later, he married again and seems to be very happy to this day.

On my return to Austria I asked what reply the Carinthian fortune-teller had given to my questions. He had predicted that in the future I should live in the Tropics and would need to brush up my English. He had also said that I should have no children. I had had a miscarriage during my marriage to Ziebel which affected me so badly that when I had recovered, I decided to attend a course designed to teach women who were living in an isolated spot with no nearby doctor or nurse to call in, how to look after their baby. Now, learning of the fortune-teller's predictions, I determined not to be influenced by them and had all my dresses made so that they could be let out if I became pregnant. I sailed for Kenya in March 1938.

On the day of our departure the radio announced Hitler's invasion of Austria. This terrible news overshadowed what seemed to me an endless journey. It was not until I saw Peter waiting for me on the quay at Mombasa that I became happy again.

He had a wonderful surprise for me; he had got a post as botanist to the Nairobi Museum and we were to have a unique honeymoon. The museum had recently received a grant for a three months' expedition to explore the Chyulu Hills. A team from the museum had just begun to do research on this unexplored area; Peter was with it and I had been invited to join him.

The Chyulu Hills are a volcanic range twenty-eight miles long, on the border of Kenya and Tanzania, half-way between Mombasa and Nairobi. Because this is a waterless area it had only been visited occasionally by a few local tribesmen poaching buffalo and antelope. The hills were of recent formation being about a thousand years old, they were unique in that the north-western area was near-barren lava and the lapilli-covered slopes of the craters were almost devoid of life. Even in these craters humus had hardly begun to collect and was barely sufficient to sustain the beginnings of vegetation. Towards the south-eastern end of the range conditions improved and there was dense rain-forest inhabited by a rich fauna. Thus, on this single range, one could study the development of vegetation and of the forms of life that depend on it.

So far I had camped on short trips with Ziebel, during which our tents were merely cover for a night. Living under canvas for three months in tents spacious enough to provide living accommodation for a zoologist, a palaeontologist, an entomologist, a geologist and a botanist was something new to me. And as well there was a field laboratory, a storage hut for food supplies and a kitchen – not to mention quarters for the staff and the porters.

The base, from which some one hundred and fifty porters collected our provisions and mail, was Kibwezi railway station.

We spent our first night near there on a large sisal estate. Here we met MacArthur, the Game Warden of the area. He was a man in his forties, with a great love of life and a sense of humour.

Also, he was a very efficient Game Warden and was toying with a plan to create a National Park with a lodge half way between Mombasa and Nairobi. His dream of starting a Game Park eventually came true when Tsavo East and West were established in 1948, but before then he had built a pub called Mac's Inn, which is now familiar to many visitors as Mtito Ndei Lodge.

Mac told us about a recently active volcano at the south-eastern end of the Chyulu Hills and of apparently bottomless vents nearby, in which poachers used to dispose the evidence of their crimes. Later, when we wrapped stones in petrol-soaked paper which we lit and then dropped down the vents, we realised how deep they must be, for we never heard the impact of the stones reaching the bottom.

Thirty-eight years later I climbed to the top of this volcano known as 'Sheitani', Swahili for devil. The lava flow had ceased but the crust of the carefully marked path on which I walked sounded alarmingly hollow, and there were prohibited areas, suggesting that the volcano was not yet extinct.

On our way from Kibwezi to the Chyulu Hills we crossed fields covered with the dry stalks of sugar cane; these had been left by the local Wakamba tribesmen before the recent drought which had ruined their crop.

The porters had gone ahead with the drinking water and after struggling across difficult ground our thirst became unbearable. To help us the guide led us to some old elephant spoor. These depressions held a little liquid which looked like thick lentil soup, but was in fact the remains of the last rains. He suggested we should collect it, boil it and drink it. It looked revolting but short of following his advice we were likely to collapse from thirst, so we drank the repulsive liquid and, because we had boiled it, we suffered no ill effects. This experience taught me never again to set out on a long expedition without carrying water, and later when people asked me what I considered the most important thing in life, obviously expecting me to say health or happiness, I invariably replied: water.

When we arrived at the camp, which was on the north-eastern end of the range, I was introduced to the Director of the museum, Dr Van Someren, and to his team. By then Peter had decided

that my Christian names, Friederike Victoria, were too complicated to pronounce and had re-christened me Joy, which has been
my name ever since.

Our camp was near the only fresh-water spring along the twenty-
eight-mile range but it was a mere trickle that took twenty-four
hours to fill one four-gallon can. We had, therefore, to be very
economical with water and washing was reduced to sponging.

I shall never forget my first breakfast in camp. The cook put
our bacon and eggs down where he could in a tent which was
full of plant presses, killing bottles and other paraphernalia.
At that moment an entomologist was dissecting a lizard. He had
pushed his jar of alcohol, filled with small dead reptiles, to one
side and as he did so the mouth of a chameleon he had recently
killed opened to evacuate the gas from its stomach. The entomologist did not notice what was happening but as for me, I
hardly had time to dash from the tent before evacuating my
stomach. Later I became accustomed to such incidents.

To make myself useful, I sketched some of the plants which
Peter had collected. This was the first time I had used water
colour and the results disappointed me. I tore the sketch up but
Peter, himself a meticulous painter of flowers, collected the pieces,
stuck them together with Scotch tape and encouraged me to go
on. I still have this first attempt at flower painting to remind me
how a hobby soon developed into one of my main interests.

Peter and I spent our days together collecting the meagre
vegetation that grew on the barren lapilli-covered slopes of the
hills and digging trenches in the floor of the crater to see how
deep the humus had collected and what plants were rooting there.

Although the hills were not more than 7,000 feet high, they
were often covered by a heavy mist that soaked our clothes.
Timber was scarce and in the evening we sat round a paraffin
stove (which Peter had brought to dry his plants) in order to keep
warm. But such discomforts were more than offset by my
initiation into a fascinating new world. Dr Van Someren had
collected many birds, each a perfect example of mutation. When
one looked at the first and last of a number of birds in a row,
one could hardly believe that they belonged to the same species,
unless one observed the gradual change of colour in individual

birds due to aging, the mating season, or varying environments.

From Dr Van Someren, I learned that many of the pigments of birds' feathers are not fast colours. He proved this by dipping the dark red feathers of a turaco into water for a few days and exposing them to the sun, with the result that they faded to a pale pink.

Ornithology was certainly thrilling but I knew that it was not for me because I realised that an ornithologist needs to kill a great many birds, and I loved living birds too much.

I often watched the entomologist dissecting insects. He explained that there could never be a hybrid crossing of two species, however nearly they might be related; this is because each microscopic genitalia has a different shape and could, therefore, not fertilise any species but its own. I admired the camouflage design of butterflies which, when they folded their wings, could give the appearance of leaves, and also that of the small groups of flattid bugs which, when they placed themselves along a stalk of grass, could simulate a flower and thereby evade their enemies.

After a month we moved camp and went to the centre of the range; although there was no ground water, the vegetation was normal for the altitude and Peter and I collected more plants than there was room for in the presses.

Drinking water here was most precious because it had to be carried ten miles from the spring to supplement the weekly supply from Kibwezi. When that arrived the peaceful stillness of the camp was broken by the noisy chatter of the porters who, in spite of the heavy loads they had to carry, were always cheerful.

They seemed almost to worship Peter and obeyed his orders with more alacrity than those given by anyone else, even though the other members of the team were much more experienced in handling Africans. This puzzled us until we discovered that Peter's prestige was due to the fact of his being left-handed – the Wakamba believe that the lion kills with its left paw and this suggested to them that Peter was endowed with equal strength. His other asset was that he sometimes wore a monocle – this the porters equated with untold wealth.

The Wakamba were the only tribe in Kenya who decorated their wooden utensils with carvings. They attached great value to them and very rarely sold a ladle, a comb or a totem-animal. To acquire one involved many hours of persuasive bargaining, yet in less than thirty years Wakamba carvings have been commercialised and today they line the pavements of Nairobi, London, Stockholm and New York. Each bears the stamp endorsing its Wakamba origin. The figures are mass-produced and lack the individual touch of the early carvers. I sometimes wonder whether the spirit which compels an artist to express himself tends to degenerate once his work has become a money-spinner.

Moving to the south-eastern end of the range we camped on the edge of the rain-forest. When leaving the blazing sun to enter its dimly lit jungle I felt as if I were walking under a cool dome supported by strange pillars. The roof was so thick that hardly a flicker of sunlight penetrated it, while the moisture exhaled by the profuse vegetation could not evaporate and dropped from leaf to leaf until it reached the ground, which was a spongy mass of decayed vegetation.

The silence of this world of timeless growth was overwhelming and was broken only occasionally by the crashing of a branch or the forlorn cry of a bird.

We had to enter the forest step by step cutting a narrow path ahead of us. Peter's method of sampling the vegetation was to stretch ropes thirty feet into the undergrowth on either side of the path and then count every plant along the rope. When we wished to collect flowers growing at the tops of the trees we often had to shoot them down with a bow and arrow of a type which Peter had designed.

There could not have been a greater contrast than that between our present studies in the rain-forest and our investigation near our first camp of the sparse humus and the few plants rooted on it. Here we were never able to find humus because it only existed deep below the decaying vegetation.

Although the atmosphere inside the forest was so damp, our water problem was worse than ever and we had to resort to sweeping sheets, in the early morning, across the dew-soaked

Joy's painting of *Gloriosa virescens*

Joy's painting of a Njemps youth

grass and then wringing them out into containers.

The Wakamba porters came to our rescue by drawing our attention to a small tree whose bitter, sticky juice, when it was decaying, turned into pure drinking water. Peter identified it as the wild banana (*Musa*) tree. From one such tree alone we obtained forty-eight gallons of liquid. This not only resolved our drinking problem but also saved our linen, which had become very brittle; now we could wash it.

As I walked daily with Peter over the difficult ground, absorbed in our search for plants and at times startled by a confrontation with a buffalo or some other wild beast, I became aware of a sensation of discomfort which I attributed to the physical effort I was making. For as long as I could, I put up with the pain but finally I could no longer walk and soon afterwards had another miscarriage. Was the Austrian fortune-teller going to be proved right in the end? I was deeply distressed.

When Peter and I returned to Nairobi Dr Jex-Blake, who had been the editor of *Gardening in East Africa* and was at this time collecting material for a second edition, and his wife, Lady Muriel, asked me to show them my flower paintings. I was rather embarrassed as I did not think they were good enough to be shown to anyone, let alone to such an expert as Lady Muriel. She was famous as the owner of a magnificent garden in Wiltshire; she had founded the Horticultural Society of Kenya and in Nairobi had made a remarkable garden filled with the indigenous plants of East Africa. I dreaded the moment when I should have to show my paintings to them, but I could not avoid doing so.

The Jex-Blakes examined them for a long time and then asked me whether I would illustrate *Gardening in East Africa*. I had only just begun painting and I did not see how I would ever be able to carry out this commission. Indeed, at the time, I felt more terrified than qualified. The commission would involve selecting plants from sea-level to high mountain flora; it would also mean keeping to a date and if I were to fail, there would be no time to get someone to replace me. I explained my panic but the Jex-Blakes were understanding and persuaded me to go ahead. From this first meeting a long friendship developed. I illustrated the second edition of *Gardening in East Africa* and also its successors.

In all, I illustrated seven books on the flora of East Africa including some on trees and shrubs.

Lady Muriel, who was a contemporary of Oma's, had much in common with her. She had the same warm nature, the same wisdom and the same capacity to bring out the best in me and she offered me moral support. This I sometimes needed as I had a difficult time adapting myself to the British code of self-control. Whereas in Austria emotional outbursts were quite acceptable – indeed a positive asset – here they were regarded with distaste. Also, because Peter was a Swiss and I was an Austrian, though people were very friendly we were naturally regarded as foreigners and I felt a sense of isolation.

To boost my self-confidence, Lady Muriel arranged for my paintings to be exhibited at Nairobi. They were well received and a few years later she insisted that I should show them at the Royal Horticultural Society's exhibition in London. This earned me the Grenfell Gold Medal and I was even offered a post as an official flower painter to Kew Gardens. This I refused because my home was now in Kenya.

As soon as we returned from the Chyulu Hills, Peter gave me a Cairn terrier puppy. It was love at first sight between us and Pippin became my best friend. We took him on every safari, covering him with mosquito nets when we were in tsetse fly infected country where he might have caught sleeping-sickness.

Pippin was a great singer, when I sang he joined in – if I raised my voice, he howled at a high pitch and if I lowered it, so did he. To amuse our friends we developed a turn in which I would howl out the 'Volga Boat Song' or an aria from *Aida*, whereupon Pippin, standing on my knees, would tune in so perfectly that our duets became famous.

Before starting to climb Mount Kilimanjaro Peter and I went for three weeks, on behalf of the museum, to a very hot area where he collected a valuable medical plant. Such herbs he always eventually sent to the Ciba or Sandoz laboratories where, after various tests, the final product ended up on sale to the public.

While we were away there were a few cases of bubonic plague in Kenya and on our return to Nairobi we were obliged to be inoculated. The three injections were usually given at a few days' interval, but to do this would have delayed my plan to climb Mount Kilimanjaro with our friend, Thomas, the botanist of the Entebbe Gardens near Kampala in Uganda, so I had the total plague vaccine in one go and suffered no ill effects.

To climb Kilimanjaro, most people start from the tiny village of Marangu in Tanzania and it was here that I met Thomas. We had been told that the climb would take three days and that we should need to hire not only a guide, but also seven porters. To keep us going we bought raisins, nuts and chocolates in preference to the heavy hard-boiled eggs, cooked meat and cheese that the hotel provided. On the first morning of our trek we walked through dense forests, where giant heather grew to fifteen feet high, lianas made thick curtains and tree ferns fanned their fronds along the banks of small mountain streams.

The flora fascinated us but we had to make do with taking notes as the porters already had their packs full. By noon we reached the Bismarck hut which stands at 8,000 feet. It had been built by Germans before the First World War and though spacious was very uncomfortable, containing only a few wooden benches and no amenities. I was all for going on but we were told that it would be wise to acclimatise ourselves slowly to the altitude. We, therefore, spent the rest of that day botanising and bird-watching around the hut.

After a cold and sleepless night we started off very early; our first stretch was through forests, then we came out on to moorland. It was lucky for us that previous climbers had made a well-trodden path, if not we should have had some difficulty in walking across the tussocks.

The most spectacular plant was the candle-like giant lobelia, of which we saw several species. Standing stiffly, and still frozen in the dawn, these plants harboured within their flowers some very rare mites which the entomologist of Nairobi Museum had asked me to collect for him. I found that all I needed to do was to shake the lobelias' five-foot-high stems and let the insects fall right into my killing bottle.

Another striking plant we saw was the giant groundsel (*Senecio*). We spent our time making notes on all the plants we recognised and had an interesting day beneath the towering, snow-capped peak of Kilimanjaro.

At noon on the second day we reached Peter hut which stands at 12,000 feet. It was even less comfortable than its predecessor. Here we remained for the rest of the day. The air was crisp and invigorating, the view across the land below glorious. The banks of a little stream were carpeted with tiny flowers, whose colours were intense.

On the third morning we approached the saddle which lies between Kilimanjaro and Mawenzi. The latter has a ragged cone which, if its crater were still intact, would be much bigger than Kilimanjaro and provides a challenge to mountaineers. Kilimanjaro is much easier to climb, neither ropes nor ice picks are needed and anyone who can stand up to the thinness of the oxygen at 19,700 feet can reach its summit.

The saddle was sparsely covered with brittle grass, we were therefore surprised to see the spoor of eland, the largest African antelope which weighs up to 1,500 lbs. We did not see any sign of other wildlife. By now we had begun to feel that the mountain belonged to us alone so we were astonished when three men appeared. They were tall, sturdy-looking Americans and alarmed us by saying that they had not been able to reach the crater, let alone the summit. This piece of news was particularly worrying for Thomas who had a weak stomach.

The Kibo hut stands at 16,000 feet; we arrived there at tea-time and went to bed early. We had been told that at this altitude we were likely to develop mountain sickness and would certainly have no appetite, but this was not the case – on the contrary, we tucked into our light, digestible provisions and felt as happy as could be. Above us the clear outline of the mountain provided an irresistible challenge and I could hardly wait till midnight when we were to begin our ascent. We had chosen midnight because that would give us a chance of reaching the crater before the ice began to melt and walking became much more difficult.

Sleeping in the tiny, stuffy hut was impossible so about 10 p.m. I went out to have a look at the weather. It was a beautiful clear night and the ice-capped crater shimmered tantalisingly, high above me. But what had happened to my knees and my stomach? I could hardly stand, let alone walk. Much alarmed, I asked Thomas to give me some of the camomile that he always carried, as well as bismuth, to calm his weak stomach. The camomile had an immediate effect, my frightening symptoms disappeared and leaving the porters behind we went ahead with our guide, Johannes.

At first we walked over loose lava but the higher we climbed, the finer the lava became – almost like cinders – till finally it resembled dust and often as we took one step forward we slid two feet back. We were obliged to rest after every four steps. When we reached 18,000 feet we had to reduce our advance still further and take more frequent rests. Johannes gallantly offered to carry my camera to relieve me of even that small weight and advised me to cover my face to avoid getting burned. Half-way up the crater I saw a butterfly, it must have been blown to this high altitude by the wind.

We reached Gilman Point on the crater just as dawn was breaking. From here we had a fantastic view: all around woolly clouds blanketed the country and only the sharp outline of Mawenzi rose out of them; immediately above it floated a mirage of the crater of Kilimanjaro. It looked like a halo crowning Mawenzi. This was an extraordinary phenomenon which even Johannes, who had so often guided people up the mountain, had never seen before.

Many years ago a skeleton of a leopard was found at Gilman Point. There was nothing near there that a leopard could eat so it is to be supposed that feeling death near, he had climbed up the crater wall seeking the solitude which animals desire when they are about to die.

In the stillness of this early dawn I felt strangely exhilarated, almost buoyant. The ice was firm enough to allow us to walk round the rim of the crater to Kaiser Wilhelm Spitze. Here we wrote our names and placed the paper in a bottle provided for the purpose. This would prove that we had reached the highest point in Africa.

In the past, when climbing in Europe, I had always made a great effort to reach the top of the mountain I was attempting to scale, not because I was keen on records, but for the moral satisfaction of conquering the impulse to quit when the going got very hard. Later, I found this training in tenacity very useful in other fields.

When the light improved we looked into the crater and saw it was filled with blocks of blue-green ice of the most fantastic shapes, while below us the landscape gradually emerged from the clouds.

Soon Johannes urged us to begin our descent for if we delayed the ice would get soft. It was easy enough to go down the lava scree and when we reached firm ground I ran all the way to the Marangu Hotel, which we reached before dark. Here Johannes presented me with the traditional trophy given to all who reach the summit of Kilimanjaro; it consisted of a garland of ruby-red everlastings, which he had picked on the moorlands. I was sad to part from Johannes who had become a friend; we had spent only four days together but they had been very special days. I gave him my mountain boots as a farewell gift since his own did not seem adequate to stand up to the sharp lava and ice, but when he left with them flung over his shoulder he said he would wear them in the village on Sunday, rather than waste such fine boots on ice.

After a three-week safari in very hot country, three plague inoculations in one day, and now the strenuous climb up to 19,700 feet, I had a right to feel very tired but instead I was bursting with energy and seemed to be in great need of exercise. I was quite worried by this reaction and asked Dr Jex-Blake's advice. He told me it was normal since one's red blood corpuscles multiply to meet physical exertion – therefore, I now needed to get rid of the surplus. He also suggested that for people living in the Tropics, climbing Kilimanjaro might provide an alternative to the holiday in the cool climate, which they are expected to require every three years.

From the time I came to Kenya we became close friends of Mary and Louis Leakey, and whenever possible we joined them in their excavations in the Rift Valley. They taught me more about anthropology and archaeology than I could possibly have learned through books and it was from them that I came to know working before. Now I tried my hand at making some bowls decorated with relief and later I embossed silver plates in which I encrusted semi-precious stones, but I was in fact more interested in three-dimensional sculpture – particularly in releasing a figure from an untouched block of wood.

My first carving was of a woman holding a hare in her arms (perhaps my mind was dwelling on Hasi?). I was excited by the ingenuity needed to use the grain of the wood to enhance the movement of the figure. Now I thought I had found the medium in which I could fulfil my artistic ambition.

I was concentrating so hard on my carving that I failed to notice that Kapps had become excessively concerned about me. His marriage had never been a happy one and his companions at Saubsdorf were boring so no doubt I had brought a new interest into his life. Whilst he painted my portrait I thought he stared at me rather frighteningly and when next he told me that he would like to sculpt me in the nude, I said no and returned to Vienna.

I was eighteen, tall and slim, and in spite of a grown-up appearance, rather childish. With my turned-up nose I felt like Cinderella when compared to Traute who had beautiful features, was a great success with university students and was always invited to their parties. Personally, I thought most of the students bores and many positively revolting with their faces scarred as a result of duels; but, all the same, I did not like feeling that I was left out of the world of flirtation in which Traute, my girlfriends and even my acquaintances at the dress-making course lived.

We had dancing classes from a Madame Winkler to prepare ourselves for our first Hofburg Ball, which always took place in the Imperial Castle. I had looked forward to it immensely but when the great evening came, I thought that waltzing round in front of rows of people and trying to smile as my partner trod on my toes was a very poor form of entertainment.

The more I mixed with my contemporaries, the more aware I became that they were much more knowledgeable about sex than I was. Of course, living in the country I had seen dogs and cattle mating. But if ever I asked a question about how babies came into the world I was invariably told: 'One doesn't talk about such things,' which made me feel that there was something shameful about it. Naturally, as I grew older, I became increasingly curious but Milli, our cook, was the only person I had to enlighten me.

She was a dear but a simple peasant with rather primitive ideas about love. Later, she became pregnant, my mother sacked her and she left instantly in disgrace. Milli did not tell me what had happened but her dramatic departure was a great shock to me.

With no one left to inform me about the facts of life I sneaked into the library whenever I could and there found some books on birth and one on sex by Van der Velde. They were more informative than Milli's explanations but rather frightening so I thought it best to go no further into the subject.

Later, when I was on a skiing holiday I met a charming young Hungarian. We grew very fond of each other, then suddenly he became gravely ill and had to go away for treatment. We corresponded and when he recovered he came to Vienna to see me. We had many interests in common and he was a delightful companion but I did not feel that I loved him enough to marry him, not even when he threatened to become a priest if I would not. We parted as friends and I did not see him again for forty years. When at last we met he was happily married, had some lovely children and was still charming. We found that our friendship had remained as warm as ever, indeed it seemed to have been enriched by our maturity.

One day I asked him whether he had been hurt when I said I did not feel I could marry him. He replied that when he had come to Vienna to see me, he had certainly hoped for more than friendship, but that he had been startled to see how tall I had grown since our skiing holiday and had found it rather embarrassing to look up when he talked to me. This made me wonder why men should feel like this since, amongst animals, the male is often smaller than the female. (This is true of bees, scorpions, eagle owls and many other species.)

I had just received two proposals which I had turned down as tactfully as I could, when Traute married; this was a sudden and most unexpected event. Some friends had introduced us to a of the vital role that Kenya has played in these fields.

For the first year Peter and I lived in a boarding-house close to the museum; then his mother visited us and gave us money to build a house of our own. When the contractor we employed failed to finish his work by the date at which we expected to move in, the Leakeys came to our rescue and invited us to share the bungalow they had rented for their work.

It contained the minimum of furniture: a double bed, a table and two chairs; all the rest of the space was empty, used for reconstructing fragments of excavated bones. This was a very time-consuming work for the Leakeys, in which we tried to help in our amateurish way.

It was while we were all crawling on the floor trying to match some bone fragments to each other that the radio announced the terrible news of the outbreak of the Second World War. Fearing for my friends and relations in Austria, who were as anti-Nazi as I was, I broke down. Peter and the Leakeys did their best to comfort me.

Not long afterwards we were invited to join Mary Leakey and a young anthropologist called Trevor, who were going to dig in the Ngorongoro crater, the largest caldera in the world, which has a diameter of some eighteen miles and a lake in its centre. Trevor's early connection with the area was interesting. The first, and indeed at that time, the only settlers to have lived in the crater were two German brothers called Siedentopf. Later, having quarrelled, they moved as far apart as possible – one remaining at the base of the crater wall, below where the present lodge stands – the other living at the opposite end where a little stream provides the only water. Both Siedentopfs were unpopular with the Masai, who owned the area, because of their habit of killing wildebeests simply to eat their tongues.

One day when the two Siedentopfs were on safari the Masai attacked the wife of one of the brothers. She sent a runner to the nearest district officer, a man named Trevor. He rode to the rescue with his young son.

Mrs Siedentopf told them that many years ago people must have lived in the crater, since when she was digging her potatoes she often found fragments of pottery. This fact stuck in young

Trevor's mind. Later, after he had taken a degree in anthropology, he decided that for his thesis he would study the remains in the Ngorongoro crater and when during the Second World War he found himself assigned to a post in Ethiopia he used his first leave to excavate the site.

At the time Louis Leakey was ill so he asked Peter to carry out botanical research while Mary and Trevor did the excavating. Not only did they dig up pottery, but also skeletons and ornaments. Peter and I helped where we could. It was a very interesting experience.

The place was teeming with animals which never left it except in times of severe drought. As our camp was near the only water we were surrounded after dark by lions and other wild beasts coming to drink. I used to listen, fascinated by the extraordinary night chorus. Then, unfailingly, a hush would come – to be suddenly pierced by agonised cries and deep growls. The king of beasts had made his kill. Utter silence followed, till gradually there came the sound of animals moving, conveying that all was safe again.

By the time we returned to Nairobi, the war was making travel difficult outside Kenya. Of course, as a neutral, Peter was unable to join in the war effort, except to the extent that he did research on the edible plants which grew in arid areas, thus providing the armies fighting in the desert with a few vegetables. We spent much of our time on safaris. For the rest we lived at home at the end of Riverside Drive, an area which was then almost undeveloped. In the early morning we ran across the countryside to get exercise. I had very little housekeeping to do, I just gave the cook instructions for that day's meals.

I spent all my time with Peter in the museum, painting indigenous flowers, and when this became known, people began to bring me rare plants. I never lacked subjects to paint and these contacts, some with very interesting people, widened our circle of friends. One day Dr Sally Atsatt, of Los Angeles University, came to the museum to make some experiments with chameleons. She had already done a lot of research on them, from the Cape to Cairo, now she wanted to make a last test to discover what made these reptiles change colour.

First she placed one in a glass container and then wrapped various pieces of coloured paper round it – the chameleon did not react. Next, she dipped the container alternately into hot and cold water – the chameleon remained green. Then she made all kinds of noises – again with no result. Finally, she held a live snake close to the glass. Abruptly the chameleon's adrenalin glands began to function and his colour changed to the darkest shade of his surroundings. Snakes are, of course, the deadly enemies of chameleons.

The chameleon is greatly feared by Africans, who will never handle one because they believe these harmless creatures to be even more dangerous than snakes. This is no doubt due to the fact that when a snake swallows a chameleon it often gets its inside ripped open by the spikes on its victim's back, and if the injury is severe the snake may well die. We often tried to demonstrate the harmlessness of a chameleon by holding one in our hand, or letting it crawl over us but it was impossible to convince an African that it was not a deadly beast.

Another cause of the Africans' fear and indeed hatred of the chameleon is said to stem from an old legend which tells how God ordered the chameleon to warn the people of a forthcoming drought, but the chameleon was so slow that he did not arrive in time – consequently most of the Africans' livestock died. In fact, the belief that chameleons are slow is false. They will keep still when being observed but if left alone they disappear in a trice.

Years later, when I was painting a splendid Jackson's chameleon, I had the occasion to observe some of their curious traits. I had placed my model on a branch, that was suspended by two thin strips of cotton, across which he could not escape. I had just started sketching him when we were obliged to move 180 miles north to Marsabit. I therefore made the chameleon as comfortable as I could in a cardboard box, in which I placed plenty of food, and I took him with me.

During this time I had observed how he produced his droppings. This he did by projecting his digestive organ out of his body and dangling it until the sac was empty. While this went on he was completely defenceless and could become a prey to any predator. It seemed to me very cruel that several times a day he should have to expose himself in this way.

Later we had to move 200 miles south to a spot near where this Jackson's chameleon had been caught. Again he moved with us, and here I completed my painting and then released him back to freedom.

4

The Congo

When Sally Atsatt had finished her experiments at the museum she proposed to go to the Congo. During her stay in Nairobi we had become friends so I suggested that we should do this trip together in our Ford. Sally was delighted and a Dutch friend of ours named Meen, asked to join us. Peter, unfortunately, was too busy at the museum to come too.

The day before we set out Louis Leakey called on us to ask if he could borrow my portable sewing machine for Mary. While waiting for this to be packed up he walked round the Ford, which had recently been repainted, and made some notes. Then he asked for the full name and home addresses of Sally and Meen. These I did not know, nor could I answer his enquiry as to the exact routes we should take, since that would depend on the rains.

Next day we started off, taking one African servant, Toto, with us. Passing Lake Naivasha and then Lake Elmenteita we reached Nakuru, which is famous for its thousands of flamingoes. We did not, however, see one bird because during the recent drought the lake had dried up and was now covered with a glistening crust of salt.

We camped near the lake for the night. To Sally's surprise I placed our safari provisions and also our spare clothes on the roof of the car. The experience of previous safaris had taught me that hyenas relish not only food, but even shoes.

Next morning we made our way to the highest point that the Kenya-Uganda railway reaches between Mombasa and Lake Victoria. It is 9,800 feet high. Under normal conditions this area is some of Kenya's best farmland but due to the drought all but the forest had turned into a scorched plain: African legends tell of the existence of the Nandi bear in these parts but up to now it has never been observed. Although we had left the heights the air was still ice-cold. We passed by the Mount Elgon crater; in the caves of this extinct volcano prehistoric people have left their traces.

Next day, we reached Kakamega. Here gold was found in sufficient quantities to give rise to Kenya's one and only gold rush. By now the amount of ore had greatly diminished – nevertheless, it still attracted a number of hopeful diggers. In consequence we were surrounded by hordes of curious Africans for whom we provided an entertainment. They were very friendly but they sang throughout the night and so we got no sleep.

We wanted to spend as much time as possible in the Congo and therefore decided to hurry through Uganda, known in those days as BBB country. This stood for Bicycles, Bananas and Bibles – to which we felt they might add two more Bs for Boundless Bogs.

To go from Kenya into Uganda one is obliged to pass over the Nile at the Ripon Falls. Before crossing the bridge we were stopped at Jinja by the police who demanded to search us. As there was a war on we assumed this normal procedure, but when the search lasted for several hours, when we were stripped of our clothes and even our toilet rolls were slit open, we became very angry at being treated as spies.

Suddenly a thought flashed through my mind that this might be the consequence of one of Louis Leakey's jokes. I recalled his unusual interest in our journey and, after all, here we were three foreign women travelling from one country to another, while he was now in the C.I.D., co-opted because of his knowledge of Kikuyu. Although an idealist who sacrificed all comfort to his work, he had a taste for detective stories and was also abnormally suspicious. Most of his reports were brushed aside by his colleagues as 'Just another of Louis Leakey's jokes.' So this incident might not be out of character. On the other hand, we were friends and he knew very well where my loyalties lay so I brushed my misgivings aside.

Later we reported the incident to our various consuls and asked for an apology. After our return to Nairobi I discovered that Louis had actually been responsible for our troubles and tackled him with it. He apologised and the affair did not mar our friendship or my respect for him.

After our ordeal we continued our journey to Kampala. We had to drive through a two-mile-long swarm of locusts, which hung like a cloud above us and covered the ground. As we crushed them by driving over them they produced an oily mess which made us skid. We had, of course, closed the windows but they entered the car from the floor, and long after we had left the swarm behind us we were reminded of them by the rancid smell of their bodies burned in the engine.

We drove through tropical palm forests and papyrus-covered swamps, till we found a high spot, far from any settlement, and here we pitched our camp. It was right on the Equator and we considered it an ideal site . . . Yet in spite of the stillness we could not sleep because of the heat; occasionally the silence was broken by the humming of mosquitoes or the howling of hyenas. Sally had never heard the so-called laughter of these scavengers and thought the noise came from giggling African girls. Fearing to alarm her, I made no comment but when we heard the unmistakable roar of advancing lions I asked Toto to get into the car and turn the lights on, thinking it would frighten them away. It was not until much later that I learned that lights and fires are apt to arouse the curiosity of lions and, therefore, to attract them. We spent the rest of the night listening anxiously to the movements of the lions near the car and were glad when we were able to leave the 'ideal camping site'.

Our next night was spent at a mission station after which, driving with the utmost caution down a precipitous track, we reached Lake Bunyonyi which is hidden by steep mountain walls. The scenery was grandiose and very beautiful. In the centre of the lake was an island on which a leper settlement had been established. Here patients were treated with the then popular chaulmoogra oil. There was no access to this area except by the hair-raising track we had taken, and then, when travellers reached the lake, there was only the station's boat to take them to the

island. Luckily our mission friends had given us an introduction
to the leper staff, and we were welcomed to the settlement.
Struck by the close friendship which existed between the patients
and the medical staff and by how happy the lepers seemed to be,
we were not surprised when we were told that in many cases
ex-patients insisted on working on the island to help with those
who were still under treatment. The station gave one the impression of being a happy little colony rather than a place for outcasts.

Continuing across increasingly steep roads through bamboo
forest, we entered Ruanda Urundi, by-passing Muhavura and
two other extinct volcanoes, which are so steep that they look
like sugarloaves.

Eventually we reached the Congo frontier. Here we saw a
few red-brick houses, their curtains tied in loops. After the wild
country we had been through, they looked remarkably bourgeois
and as thick fog hid their surroundings, I could easily imagine
that we were in Belgium, where the houses present an equally
homely aspect.

The customs officer was surprised to see us and told us that
we were the first tourists to arrive since the outbreak of war.
He wished us good luck and with a few friendly formalities we
went on.

Gradually, the country became open and we reached Lake
Kivu. The loveliness of this lake was enhanced by the still active
Nyiragongo volcano. Eruptions at rhythmical intervals which
took place close to its shore were a spectacular sight especially
after dark. The lake is safe for swimming since it harbours no
bilharzia or crocodiles. We spent the night at Kisenyi, an idyllic
place right on the water-front even though we were told that
a bad type of malaria-carrying mosquito infested the area. In the
circumstances I found it surprising that no one used mosquito
nets and instead took forty grains of quinine every day, a deadly
dose – or so it seemed to me.

Next day we went along the lake, to the spot where the latest
Nyamuragira lava flow stops most traffic. We, however, were not
to be deterred and jolted on in the car till we had to halt where the
flow ended in a drop three feet deep. From this lower level the
lava flow covered twenty square miles. After trying to walk along

its edge, we returned to our car, alarmed by the crackling of the lava beneath our feet, which seemed to threaten to cave in at any moment.

We then made our way to the place where, normally, a ferry carries cars across the lake to the road which leads to Coster-mansville. However, at the moment it was not functioning. We were nevertheless lucky enough to find the owner of a dug-out canoe who, after a bit of hard bargaining, agreed to paddle us out about two miles so that we could see the place where the boiling lava flow reaches the water.

We left the car with Toto, who soon found himself surrounded by a chattering group, speaking in a language he could not under-stand. The canoe was leaking in several places and so we spent our time stuffing the holes with grass. Meanwhile, I had a most uncomfortable feeling: here were we sitting in an unstable canoe, with two gloomy gondoliers, with whom we could not com-municate. Gradually, the tension became unbearable and I even began to wonder whether we might not be going to be robbed and then thrown into the lake. No tourists had seen us board the canoe and Toto could be of no help.

To ease the situation I began to hum an old Kikuyu song which I had recently written down for Louis Leakey, who wished to include it in his book about the tribe. I had a feeling that it must be a good thing to appear happy and carefree – and surely people who sang were relaxed? Instantly our Congolese boatmen responded by singing the 'Marseillaise.' I felt a perfect fool for having thought that I must begin with something very primitive in order to set up communication between us. Once the ice was broken we continued competing with our favourite songs until the water became very hot. The actual flow of boiling lava was hidden by clouds of steam, but at regular intervals red lava blisters were thrown above the steam. Although we kept the canoe some sixty feet away from the hissing turmoil, we were shaken by each new eruption. Like us, the two Congolese stopped their jolly songs and watched in awe. All of us felt that we were witnessing one of nature's miraculous phenomenons, and we were speechless as we tried to take in the spectacle.

On our return, Sally developed icy shivers, the first and

unmistakable symptoms of malaria. We had to spend three days at the hotel before she was fit to travel again. During that time I explored the neighbourhood, looking for wild orchids and other indigenous plants. My first assurance that Sally had recovered was when I found her on the roof of our bungalow, hunting for chameleons.

We now headed for Park Albert – that enormous area which harbours virtually all African animals with the exception of giraffes, zebras and rhinos. We drove along over a carpet of elephants' droppings to Rutshuru, a small township standing at the entrance to the park.

The elephants of the Congo have a reputation for being more aggressive than their Kenyan cousins, they have even been known to turn cars over – so we were relieved to reach Camp Ruindi without meeting one of these monsters.

Here we engaged a guide for no one is allowed to drive inside the park on their own. We went first to Lake Edward. Man-high elephant grass bordered the road. The lake was an ideal home for water birds, crocodiles and hippos. Their snorts and goggling eyes were at first the only sign of their presence, for their bulky bodies were concealed below the surface of the water. But when our guide threw some pebbles into the lake the huge beasts immediately rose, bumping into each other, then sank back after a few minutes to resume their lethargic existence. While we watched the commotion herons and pelicans glided peacefully near to these apparently harmless giants (the second largest land animals) but everybody here knew that should some person block their way back to the water after they had been grazing, they would become extremely savage. This is especially true if a cow hippo is accompanied by her calf.

On our return to Ruindi we passed many elephants plodding towards the lake to drink. The young were in the centre of the herd, well protected, while the leading elephant guarded the whole family with ears spread out. This is their charge position but our guide assured us that in this instance it was only bluff. I was very thankful that we had an experienced man with us who would be able to warn us if an elephant meant business. When it got dark we could just make out grey silhouettes, moving

Lake Rudolf

Reticulated giraffe near Isiolo

Amboseli with Mount Kilimanjaro

Tsavo West

noiselessly through the forest. To me it is unbelievable how silently these huge animals can move.

At dawn we set off with our guide and saw great herds of antelopes and many clumsy hippos enjoying the dew-covered expanse that the sun would later turn to dry straw. In the distance we glimpsed two lions on a kill. They were in grass so high that all we could observe were a couple of heads bobbing up at intervals, no doubt to keep a watchful eye on us. Then a hyena came lumbering around the car. Perhaps he was hoping to get some scraps from our lunch but he must have realised that we were not about to eat and strolled on towards the lions.

As we went on in the direction of the Rutshuru River we were nearly hit by a rumbustious buffalo who bounded comically around in the early morning sunshine. When we reached the river the hippos were enjoying their morning game but the moment they saw us they sank below the water. It was not long, however, before a pair of eyes or twitching ears reappeared and then, after a pebble or two had been thrown, their huge, glistening bodies went into action and the water churned as the hippos clambered over each other, blowing spray and grunting loudly.

We saw several buffaloes standing out in the hot sun, apparently enjoying the heat. This surprised me as the buffaloes of Kenya always keep under cover. I wondered if this might be because buffaloes are much hunted in Kenya and therefore need to conceal themselves, but feel safe in the Park Albert.

The sun was now fierce, most animals found cover and we were looking forward to a cool rest in the camp, but when we learned that our next route was through a waterless area we realised that we had no choice but to leave at once, so that we might reach the next water before dark.

Our drive took us high up along the escarpment that surrounds the plains of Park Albert like a wall. Only baboons and vervet monkeys hopped across the very narrow road, squatting as soon as they had crossed it to watch us with great interest.

After many hairpin bends we reached the park's boundary. As far as we could see there were three-foot-high ferns that gradually led to a rain-forest. The road had been blasted through rocks.

Crossing the rain-forest next morning we saw tree ferns, palms, giant lobelias, man-high orchids and highly coloured creepers inextricably mingled. This was a tantalising sight as we had no time to stop and collect specimens.

When we reached the small settlement of Lubero, African children offered us baskets of delicious-looking wild strawberries. I was sorry to refuse them but I remembered how a friend of mine had bought just such tempting baskets in Cairo and enjoyed them, until the day when she happened to walk down a side lane and see a number of Egyptians squatting in a line as they licked the dust off their strawberries before offering them for sale.

After a while we came to a little rest-house standing in a wilderness. It was spotless and a typical Austrian *Dirndl* welcomed us. She owned this charming chalet and since she came from Salzburg we discovered that we had many mutual interests. After eating splendid *Wiener Schnitzel* and *Salzburger Nockerl* we regretfully drove on to Beni, a village with just one street, in which there were the usual Indian shops and a few bungalows owned by Europeans. We were not attracted to the shabby hotel and went on another twenty miles to a guest house said to be very comfortable and not far from the Pygmy settlements which we hoped to visit. The Africans we saw were almost naked. The men walked proudly, balancing their spears. The women carried heavy loads of grass or wood on their heads and each had her youngest baby tied by a cloth to her back. The older children scampered around their mothers; the boys, even small ones, carried little spears. By the side of the road were some mud huts, where old women crouched round fires, smoking long pipes.

When at last we arrived at the 'comfortable guest house' it proved to be a musty, smelly, one-roomed affair with a mud floor covered with animal spoor and crawling with insects. We decided to sleep in the car, even though it was oppressively hot and we dared not open a window because of the stream of chattering Africans who surrounded us for most of the night. Toto added to the clamour by shouting repeatedly: 'Go away, my master wants to sleep!' Sally and I kept very quiet, not wishing to betray the fact that his 'master' was in fact three women who were only too happy to have Toto's masculine voice for protection.

At dawn we were woken by strange giggling, quite different from the previous chatter and when we emerged from the car saw a group of dwarfs, their skinny legs supporting enormous bellies, which in the case of the women were partly covered by long, flat, pendant breasts – proof that they had nursed many babies; these were the Pygmies. We thought they looked nightmarish.

Their faces were covered with wrinkles and apart from the classic fig leaf they were naked. Watching them peeping into our car and looking at our strange belongings, it seemed to us that these little people had come from another world.

We had brought tobacco with us and now distributed it among the Pygmies. Immediately they offered us two of their tiny bows, wrapped in monkey skin to give a better grip, and two tiny arrows, their points dipped in poison so deadly that it could kill a lion within minutes. We accepted our dangerous presents very carefully and after taking some photographs, parted on the most friendly terms. Contrasting their great generosity in giving us two of their most cherished possessions and the courage with which they will hunt large beasts such as elephants for food, against their repulsive ugliness (which caused Toto to ask if these creatures could really be Africans), I decided that on balance they were most endearing people. Later, when I had an opportunity to study them over a much longer period, this impression was confirmed.

We went on to cross the hanging bridge over the Semliki River, where we saw many crocodiles but looked in vain for the peaks of the Ruwenzori, which were covered with thick cloud. Ever since the time of Ptolemy people have tried to discover the secrets of these Mountains of the Moon, which are non-volcanic; yet, even today, comparatively little is known about their flora, fauna or ecology.

Driving up the slopes as far as was possible we tried to catch a glimpse of the forest that covers the route leading to the moorland. Having found an old track, we jolted along it for two hours, crossing streams and going round rocky outcrops till we came to a small plateau, on which stood a mud hut surrounded by a garden. To our great surprise, a white man in his sixties suddenly appeared and graciously invited us to lunch. Intrigued, we accepted, feeling sure that our host would prove to be an interesting character – as indeed he did. Colonel Harcass had built himself this little retreat for his old age, and here he lived with his African staff and a chimpanzee for company. Before his retirement he had spent thirty years pioneering in the Belgian Congo.

Behind the house was a waterfall; its water was so pure that one could drink from it without fear. Beyond the waterfall the rain-forest disappeared into clouds, while in front of the house there was a splendid view over Park Albert, Lake Edward and beyond to a sea of forest-clad hills. The general effect was one of remoteness and of peace and freedom.

During the last nine years Colonel Harcass had built some roads to open up the area. More importantly, it was largely due to his work that the park had been freed of sleeping-sickness, which in the past had claimed thousands of victims each year.

There were a large number of albino tribesmen in the region. With their white hair, light skin and reddish eyes, they looked most unlike the local Africans and found themselves at a disadvantage. The Colonel had helped them to find work. Recently he had started a new project by setting up an okapi farm to protect these rare cousins of the giraffe, which were much in demand by zoos and in great danger from poachers. We were also shown photographs and publications about expeditions to the six Ruwenzori mountains, and admired many unknown birds, butterflies, reptiles and small mammals – mostly collected by our host. All had been carefully preserved so that when the war ended they could be sent to Brussels for identification.

After a lunch which would have earned praise from any gourmet, the Colonel presented us each with an elephant's tail; we then left our kind host to the company of his Africans and his chimpanzee. We never heard of him again.

At sunset we reached the Congo-Uganda border, and were delighted when the Belgian customs officer offered us the use of his guest house. He treated us to a wide selection of duty-free drink, followed by roast wild pig (my first), washed down with French wines (incidentally, alcohol here was much cheaper than

68

water, which had to be carried over many miles). A party inevitably followed this excellent meal; it ended with all of us singing our favourite songs to the accompaniment of a zither. For a while we forgot about the war and our differing countries of origin. But the greatest surprise came when we retired for the night to find rows of buckets of hot water awaiting us in our bathroom – and what a room that was! In the middle stood a cement bath about nine feet square; we thought it was perhaps meant for a family. Anyway, we were most grateful for this luxury, the more so knowing how scarce water was.

The next morning our amiable host insisted on himself opening the customs barrier for us. We waved our prized elephants' tails in farewell and were puzzled to see him turn his head away. It was not until later that we learned that a very heavy fine was imposed on all owners of such illegally acquired trophies.

On we drove through forests of candelabra euphorbias and saw many succulents, some of which I collected for Peter who specialised in them. While I was digging them up a crowd of Africans gathered. They wore clothes of bark-cloth, which is ochre-coloured. It is made by beating the bark of a certain tree for so long that it becomes paper thin but very hard-wearing.

After passing Kampala and then the Nile at the Ripon Falls we reached Kisumu, a small town that nestles in the bed of what in prehistoric times was the full extent of Lake Victoria, an area of 68,450 square miles. When later I teased Peter, saying that it was four times the size of Switzerland, he replied patriotically: 'Not if you iron out Switzerland.'

The final lap of our journey was across the highlands of Kisii and Kericho, where we saw acres of the neatly cropped bushes of Kenya's largest tea plantations. This lush region was followed by the straw-coloured plains that led us back to Nairobi.

5

I Meet George

Kenya was now threatened by the Italian Forces occupying Ethiopia. It was thought they might attack at any moment, so a defence force known as the Reckies, and consisting chiefly of farmers, was raised.

One morning when I was at home painting a very rare white delphinium, which Lady Muriel had brought me, the door opened and a policewoman accompanied by an escort appeared. She told me to pack such essentials as I needed because I was going to be detained for the duration of the war.

Peter and I were stunned. It had never occurred to us that my Austrian origin would bring suspicion upon me since everyone knew of my detestation of both Nazis and Fascists.

We insisted that there must be some mistake – but in vain. My plea to be allowed to finish the painting I was working on was met by the remark that I could take the flower with me to the convent, where I and other suspects were to be housed until a permanent camp had been set up.

I packed and carrying Pippin under my arm, followed the police-woman to the convent. There I found women of many different nationalities, including some Britons, all chattering in their own tongues. My arrival, holding the white delphinium in one hand and carrying a dog under my other arm, caused some surprise. I was asked how it had come about that I had been allowed to bring Pippin. I replied that he was not just a dog, he was my friend. Then I retreated into a corner and continued painting. Concentrating on the exquisite blue stamen and frail lacy petals took me into a world in which no human being could hurt me.

Next morning we were all taken by train to the highlands and housed in a farm that stood at an altitude of 8,000 feet. Our living conditions were extremely primitive. We shared a feeling of great depression but this was about the only thing we had in common. I was very glad that I was allowed to sketch flowers growing around the camp. In the hurry of our departure I had forgotten to pack Pippin's feeding dish. So, as there was no spare crockery, I carved a small bowl for him out of a piece of firewood – but what food was I to put in it?

Sharing my rations with him in no way satisfied his appetite. Fortunately, by then he had endeared himself to some of my fellow prisoners, who passed a little of their food to him under the table. Every morning we were lined up and made to do exercises. When Pippin first saw us hopping and skipping, he looked bewildered, then he took to imitating us – jumping when we jumped, and when we ran in circles accompanying us. Even our severe instructress had to chuckle.

Peter did everything in his power to discover the reason for my arrest. What he learned was that the C.I.D., knowing of my friendship with the Jex-Blakes, had gone round to see them and asked them about my visitors. In all innocence, they mentioned that they had sometimes met German-speaking people at our house. These friends were in fact German-speaking Swiss, but it was because of this misunderstanding that I had been arrested.

When the Jex-Blakes learned what had happened they went to the Governor and asked that I should be released immediately. He agreed and when I reached home after one week I gave Lady Muriel my painting of the white delphinium as a proof that nothing could impair our friendship.

Soon after my return Peter became seriously ill with kidney trouble. When he was well enough to travel his doctor suggested that he should have a complete break. Since it was impossible to fly to Europe he decided to go to South Africa. I was very sad not to be able to go with him, especially as he was so unwell.

During his absence I accepted an invitation to stay with Alys Reece, the wife of the officer in charge of the Northern Frontier

Province, an area of 120,000 square miles. I was to help her with her children – two little girls of four and five and a boy of four who was staying with them.

I met Gerald and Alys Reece at Isiolo, a few days before they had moved to Marsabit to avoid the worst of the heat. In those days it was a small village consisting of a few Somali *dukas* (shops) and the offices and residential quarters of the officers in charge, a district commissioner, a superintendent of police and his men, and a livestock inspector. The headquarters of the Game Warden was eight miles out in the hills, as from there it was easier to get information about poachers.

Isiolo is sited at an altitude of 3,000 feet and is very hot when the wind blows, shifting sand from the plain across it. The plain is immense, framed in the far distance by mountain ranges.

While Alys Reece was introducing me, at the tennis courts, to the families of some of the officials I was fascinated by the little volcanoes, a few inches high, which mole-rats were busy throwing up all over the courts, even as play went on. I was told that they belonged to a rare species, naked and with a skin so transparent that their whole anatomy is visible through it. They live only in hot and arid country.

As well as being the HQ of the Northern Frontier administration Isiolo was also the gateway into this forbidden province. Symbolically a barrier had been erected across the road, past which nobody could go without a permit. A few hundred yards further up, the road forked – one branch leading to Abyssinia via Marsabit, the other to Somalia via Wajir. These were the only roads suitable for motors through this semi-desert country. To me it seemed that the wooden barrier was not just an obstacle placed in the way of trespassers but that it was a barrier between life lived by man according to the laws of civilisation, and the unpredictable life of untamed nature – cruel but of boundless grandeur. I was determined that one day I would travel far beyond the mountains which I saw on the horizon.

Our packing finished, we set off on the 180-mile drive to Marsabit; it led along the Mathews Range till we reached the Kaisut Desert. Here the lorries had some difficulty in crossing a few dry river beds. Later we climbed up the slopes of Marsabit, making our way towards the forest. Many volcanic hills dotted the northern slope and were even to be seen as far down as Kaisut. The highest mountain was merely 4,000 feet but when the monsoon blew from the coast this was the first obstacle it met with and, as a result, the upper slopes of the volcanic mass received sufficient moisture to develop a rich vegetation. In the forest flags of grey lichen floated from every tree, and the under-growth was dense.

I was told that the only permanent water came from a small spring in the heart of the forest, where a cascade fell over rocks to form a pool which was the life blood of both men and beasts.

The Reeces had built two small log huts at the top of a hill near the forest and here they spent the few hot months during which they left Isiolo.

The view across the desert to the north and far away to Lake Rudolf was so vast that I wished I had wings to help me explore it.

When we had settled in I went for a walk to stretch my legs after the long drive. On my return Gerald asked me where I had been. I pointed to a dark line on the plain below, remarking: 'Along that cattle track.' 'That,' he replied smiling, 'is the main road to Moyale, an outpost some hundred miles away on the Abyssinian border.'

During my visit I tried, as arranged, to help with the children; the first task of the day was to take them for a walk soon after dawn, while breakfast was being prepared.

After the meal Alys gave them lessons while I painted flowers, with a hot-water bottle on my lap to warm my frozen fingers. The flowers, of which there were a great variety, were particularly beautiful thanks to the heavy morning mist.

The Reeces were both very keen on horses and had about twenty hardy little ponies. Bred by the Boran tribe, they coped amazingly well with the surrounding terrain dotted with ant-bear holes.

When the Boran invaded Kenya from the north some halted around Marsabit, these remained pagan; others migrated south and settled near Isiolo, these were converted to Islam. All were excellent horsemen, very good-looking and I found them a proud and lovable people.

Often Alys and I would make our way to some hill, tie the horses to a tree at its base and climb to the top. There, as we sat motionless and silent, a klipspringer or even a Greater kudu would come close. They appeared to be the only living creatures on these hills, or indeed on the boundless plain below us.

As we watched the sun getting low and turning the desert into a deep glowing red, I would look longingly at the distant outline of Mount Kulal and the faint silver streak of Lake Rudolf. How far I was then from guessing that one day this wild country was to become my home.

At this time Marsabit was an important army post, both because of its strategic positions and because it had the one fresh water spring for hundreds of miles around. In the nearby forest there were also a few hidden camps from which, in the evenings' some officers often dropped in for a chat, or listened to records, of which the Reeces had a fine collection, while we two mended their torn clothes. If the weather was warm enough, we took the gramophone into the open and enjoyed the music as we sat looking at the stars.

Having read Martin Johnson's book about Lake Paradise I wanted to visit it, but it was fifteen miles away and petrol was strictly rationed. So, the only way to get there was to go on foot through the forest.

Alys found a guide for me, and taking Pippin and her Ridgeback we set off. The forest was magnificent and, walking quietly, with the dogs on the leash, we surprised several duikers, bushbucks and other small animals. Never having seen people so deep in the forest, they let us come very close.

Suddenly the guide touched my shoulder and whispered: 'Run!' Holding on to the dogs I ran as fast as I could till I was out of breath, then I hid behind a tree. If the guide had not warned me I should have walked straight into an elephant. As it was he came after us with waving trunk and wide-spread ears. There were some terrifying moments, then the guide shouted: 'Let the dogs go, he's only after them!' I could not bear to risk

Pippin so I grabbed him but I did unleash the ridgeback, who dashed off yapping and sure enough the elephant swerved towards him. To my great relief the dog returned to us in a short time, no worse for the chase, and the elephant disappeared but the guide said we must turn back if we were to avoid more elephants, for he had seen a lot of droppings about. This was the first time I had encountered an elephant on foot. It had certainly been a frightening experience. Yet I felt that in a way it was an initiation to a life towards which I was strangely drawn.

One day we learned that a battalion, coming from across the border on its way to Nairobi, would pass by the Reeces' house. Knowing that many of the officers were good horsemen we decided to organise a steeple-chase, but as there were not enough horses – camels, mules, donkeys, anything that had four legs and was large enough to mount was co-opted and to add to the fun, we had to have drinks. But as we were rationed to one bottle of whisky a month, we had to make our own beer. Alys was quite an expert in mixing jaggery into the brew and knew exactly when to stop the fermenting process to guarantee a delicious and rather potent drink. The officers, used to ample Naafi supplies, could hardly conceal their disappointment at being offered home-made beer, but accepted it out of courtesy. Later they could not get enough of our mead and had the best steeple-chase of their lives. Needless to say – a donkey won.

While I was at Marsabit Peter's letters had been most encouraging. It seemed he was making a speedy recovery and he was already planning a safari to Lake Rukwa, where he hoped to find a rare plant. We were to meet near Lake Victoria and from there continue on foot. Gerald Reece gave me a lift back to Isiolo. When we arrived I opened the mail that was waiting for me and found a letter from a friend who had recently met one of the officers who had taken part in our steeple-chase. He had told her he was astonished that I, as an Austrian, should have been allowed to help entertain the army. I was shocked for it had never crossed my mind that I might have been an embarrassment to the Reeces. Very distressed I showed the letter to Gerald. The light was failing, he took a torch and led me to a tree whose branches were loaded down with the weight of thousands of

tiny birds, too exhausted to continue their migratory flight to
Europe. He took one of them in his hand and stroking it remarked: 'Isn't all this much more important than your letter.'

As a result of my stay at Marsabit I was in excellent form but
Peter's long walk to Lake Rukwa had tired him out.

After our return to Nairobi Lady Muriel organised an exhibition of my paintings, Lady Moore commissioned me to do
twenty flower pictures which were to be presented to General
Smuts (himself a keen botanist specialising in grasses) and, as
well, I was asked to paint flowers for table mats for the Royal
Lodge, which Kenya later presented to the Queen and Prince
Philip. Meanwhile, Peter was asked by the museum to test some
local pigments which might be useful to the army for camouflaging
tents and cars, at a time when, owing to the war, the importation
of such pigments was restricted. A road-engineer working near
Garissa had recently brought in rocks which, when crushed,
yielded chromium. He believed there were other minerals in the
area from which yellow and brown pigments could be obtained.

We joined him and his family in their large camp 100 miles
from Garissa. Peter identified several promising minerals and
also found plants from which permanent dyes could be obtained.

The Christmas season was approaching when the District
Commissioner from Garissa, Willy Hale, passed by the camp and
invited us to spend the holidays with him. We accepted. In 1942
Garissa was a small outpost with a district commissioner and a
police inspector and his force; there were no other Europeans
living there. As the altitude was only 1,000 feet it was very hot,
the houses had been built with thick walls, and at sunset everyone
moved onto the flat roofs. The Tana, Kenya's largest river,
flows close to Garissa; it has a pontoon bridge, by which all
traffic crosses the crocodile-infested water. The thickly wooded
banks were the home of many elephants, smaller game and birds.
There were also a few rice fields which supplied the small population of Somali and Riverine tribes with their main food.

The Hales told us that this Christmas would be a special
one because they had invited more Europeans than ever before.
Besides Morna and Willy Hale, Peter and myself – a livestock

inspector, a police inspector and George Adamson from the Game Department, who was still on a camel safari in the North – were expected. Morna and I began preparing a feast. As we did so she told me about the other guests, in particular about George Adamson, a legendary figure who had had many adventures.

One morning he had been mauled by a lioness and only rescued by his men many hours later. A few days before the Game Department had sent him some sulphanilamide, a new drug said to counteract blood poisoning. After washing his wounds with Epsom salts, he told his men to give him a capsule of sulphanilamide every four hours. Later, suffering from malaria, as well as from loss of blood, he became delirious, but woke up during the night to see a rogue elephant charging straight at his tent. He yelled to the cook to prop him up and taking his gun, fired, killing the giant with a shot through the brain. This sensational event had made a hero of him.

On Christmas Eve our party were sitting on the parapet of the flat roof dressed in our Sunday best; I was wearing a long silver evening-gown that was quite out of place in Garissa. A crowd of Somali and Riverine tribesmen had gathered round the house all set for a big *ngoma* (dance) when, suddenly, they scattered and a line of camels appeared with George Adamson riding at their head. After a quick bath he joined us on the roof. Willy Hale offered him a stiff whisky, then a second, then a third. By now Morna and I showed some concern, but George said defiantly: 'I never get tight.' That was all we needed to decide to prove him wrong. We poured brandy into his soup, into his gravy, into everything he ate. I watched him anxiously, attracted by his large blue eyes, his sun-tanned face framed by blond hair and his carefully trimmed goatee beard.

When the moon rose, illuminating the dancing and singing tribesmen below, the mood became still more festive. Our men changed into *kikois* and one after another left us to disappear into the mob, except for George who sat on the parapet singing. When I woke next morning I found shreds of my silver dress hanging round the barbed wire that surrounded our tent. George was discovered, feeling far from well, with his boots still on and resting on the pillow, while his head was at the other end of his bed.

It was decided that Peter and I should join George's next camel safari. We would go down stream to Bura. From there George would go north while the Hales would pick us up and take us by car to Lamu, an area which Peter did not know and where he hoped to collect new plants.

Once we had left the river bank with its large trees, the country became hot and dry.

Now I, who had seldom ridden a camel before, found myself sitting on an improvised saddle made of grass matting placed between the two humps and held in position by crossed sticks. Watching from my high and comfortable seat, all that happened below, I felt like a queen. Later, when the sun got hot, I nearly fell asleep. This was delightful but when I had to get down for lunch, what with the heat of my body and the fact that my back had been continually rubbing against damp matting, I discovered that the friction had scraped the skin off my spine. My back was a bloody mass and in places the bones were visible. We used disinfectant and in time the wound healed, but for a long while I felt agonising pain when I lay on my back, and worse still when I bent down. However, the country was so fascinating that I did not feel sorry for myself and besides, Peter was finding many interesting plants and George was opening up a new world to me with his stories of wild animals.

He was a puzzle to me – very silent, which I attributed to his lonely life. Indeed, I had been prepared for this by Morna, who said laughingly that George never listened to what people said and had only three answers which covered all possible situations: 'Oh,' 'Really,' 'How extraordinary.'

We slept out under mosquito netting, tents would have been much too hot. During the night I listened to lions roaring, hyenas chuckling, to other strange animal noises and to the humming of cicadas. There seemed a challenge in learning about a world as untamed as the creatures living in it.

When we reached Bura I would have loved to go on through the bush rather than to Lamu, where there would be Arabs to see and not much else.

In the past, when slavery was customary, Lamu was the agricultural centre of the coast but since the slaves have been freed the town has degenerated into a sleepy place – a living museum with attractive inhabitants, but doomed unless the people get more educated so that they can keep up with some of the more enterprising African tribes. In its narrow streets we saw Arabs wearing white, silk, loose-flowing gowns and white, cotton, hand-embroidered caps. Some sat in their shops which mostly sold spices and hand-woven *kikois*. The women, who were still in purdah, came out after dark; they wore black cloth *bui-buis* and only their eyes showed through slits. Life in Lamu was confined to the harbour, to which dhows brought dates, spices and Persian carpets from Arabia to exchange them for Kenyan products.

Across a channel a few miles wide lay Lamu Island, part of an archipelago which stretches 100 miles north to the border of Somalia. We stayed at the District Commissioner's house which was on the water-front. It was a two-storey building surrounding a large patio, typically Arab in style. The walls were very thick, the rooms big, beautifully proportioned and the carved wooden furniture stood out strikingly against the white-washed walls. The only thing lacking in this attractive establishment was a loo. Whenever nature called one was obliged to summon a special wallah who would immediately rush up the staircase carrying a throne. Morna and I found this very embarrassing, so early one morning we went out to find a bush. What we had forgotten was that we were the only women with fair hair and blue eyes in the town, as a result we were followed by a crowd till we became desperate. Luckily, at that moment, a dhow had come up the channel and anchored by a nearby landing jetty. Morna asked the Captain to take us to an uninhabited island, and wait for us till we were ready to go back. We returned much relieved but very late for breakfast.

Soon after we got back to Nairobi George and I met quite by chance. He had not intended this to happen for, having fallen in love with me and being honourable, he had meant to avoid me so as not to jeopardise my marriage. But fate intervened and it was not long before I found myself involved in a divorce.

I needed to be alone during this distressing time so I decided to camp on the moorlands of Mount Kenya and paint the flowers there. The Equator cuts right across the ice-covered peaks of this extinct volcano, which rises to an altitude of 17,000 feet. In consequence the alpine flora of Europe grows alongside plants found in South Africa and giant lobelias and senecios which are only to be seen on the highest mountains of East Africa and the Andes.

Mount Kenya being on the border line of the two hemispheres, combines uniquely contrasting climatic conditions, for while during the European winter the northern slopes are covered with deep snow and retain a few glaciers during the European summer, the southern slopes have the reverse climate.

My idea was to camp at 14,000 feet where the forest belt ends and the moorlands begin. I found it was not an easy plan to put into operation. I would need a cook, and a gun-bearer to accompany me in my search for flowers and to keep an eye out for buffaloes and elephants. I would also need porters for we would have to have a weekly supply of mail, as well as food for the three of us, and Pippin brought up the mountain. The two district officers I approached had heavy responsibilities on account of the war and could not add to these by undertaking to look after a woman who wished to camp high up on the mountain in order to paint flowers.

It was a farmer named Raymond Hook who solved my problems. He was a curious character who had done research on the impact the Portuguese had left on Africa. He was also a great naturalist and had a surprising knowledge of the history of cheetahs – ever since they were kept as pets by the Assyrians, the Ancient Egyptians and the Mediaeval French. Hook had trained some cheetahs for Indian Maharajahs and had taken a few to England to race against greyhounds; a venture that fell flat owing to the superiority of the cheetah. He had crossed buffaloes with cattle, zebras with horses and was the first to breed a handsome zebroid, which had the stripes and head of a Grevy's zebra and the colouring of a brown horse. These he either used as pack animals or sold to zoos. A scholarly man, he lived in very primitive conditions.

He offered to send two men weekly on horseback to my camp.

They would carry our supplies. In the event they often had to turn back because of bad weather, or the presence of truculent elephants, but in the end the supplies got through, Raymond never let me down. When the men arrived they always brought little notes telling me where I would be likely to find the most interesting plants.

It was on his advice that I placed my small mountain tent, another for the two men, and a studio made of bamboo poles at the edge of the moorlands under one of the last of the forest trees. The advantage of this was that if we were invaded by elephants or buffaloes we could shin up a tree. In fact, one buffalo nightly squeezed between our two tents, rubbing himself against the canvas and terrifying Pippin.

I had chosen the rainy season to get the richest flora, snow fell daily around us and the mist didn't lift till lunch-time. It was a striking sight to see blood-red gladioli, deep-blue and turquoise delphiniums and red-hot pokers growing straight out of the snow. Smaller flowers grew along the little streams and were of a much more intense colour than those of the same species growing at a lower level. The altitude also had an effect on the fauna – elands, buffaloes, jackals and hyrax were much larger than those of the lower levels, their fur was thicker and often of a different colour but the trophies were smaller than those of the same species on the plain. The giant lobelias and senecios attracted several kinds of sunbirds, which elsewhere are never seen together.

One day the gun-bearer and I carried a nine-foot lobelia into camp as I could not paint it where it grew. Very soon I felt sick and so did the gun-bearer, whose eyelids, nostrils and lips began to swell up. Then I remembered that once when Peter had taken some sections of lobelia to press, even though afterwards he had carefully washed his hands, half an hour later when he happened to whistle through his fingers, he vomited. All lobelia contain a poisonous caustic latex, because of this it is never used as fire-wood, even on the high moorlands where there are no trees, for when ignited even the fumes cause nausea. This poison is far stronger than that of digitalis.

I had intended to spend a month on the mountain but I found so many flowers to paint that I decided to stay on. In all, sitting with a hot-water bottle on my knees and Pippin warming my feet, I sketched seventy different flowers in four months.

George came almost every weekend to visit me. On one occasion he turned up late and very exhausted, having driven 230 miles from Marsabit and completed the journey on foot up to my camp, walking in heavy rain through the dense forest where he was lucky not to meet elephants or buffaloes, whose approach he could not have seen in the dark.

He had just recovered from malaria thanks to taking large doses of mepacrine. This is a drug to which many people are allergic and it can have terrifying side effects: some people lose their memories, some become violent, others talk gibberish.

The morning after his arrival George went out to shoot the buffalo who plagued us by night. These animals seldom charge straight at a person, nevertheless, they are very dangerous, especially if wounded, for they have a habit of circling the hunter and attacking him from behind. This particular buffalo did, however, charge George who had not yet fired and he had a very narrow escape, before he was able to put a bullet through the animal's head.

On our way to camp George began to talk in a very strange way and when we reached home he yelled for his revolver, shouting that he meant to shoot the lot of us. After what seemed an endless struggle we managed to get him onto a bed where we held him down. All through the night he yelled at us and threw himself around. It was a frightening experience. Eventually, towards dawn, he fell into a deep sleep, from which he woke up weak but normal. The big doses of mepacrine he had taken were the cause of his delirium. He stayed in camp until he had completely recovered.

One weekend we circled the peaks of Mount Kenya just below the levels of the glaciers. Every valley was different in character, in most we saw blue tarns but resisted the temptation to plunge into them, recalling that several people had died of heart failure after swimming in their icy water.

Eventually the weather changed, the monsoon blew with accelerating force, crashing through the forest and felling many trees. As a consequence I eventually became a wreck due to sleep-lessness and fear that my camp might be hurled at any moment into the forest by these icy blasts.

On my way home I went to Nanyuki to see Raymond Hook and asked him what I owed him, he replied: 'I know this great mountain probably better than anyone else; now that I am too old to walk, even to the moorland, I simply wanted to help you with your painting so that your pictures can bring this beautiful flora to people who, like myself, can no longer go to see the flowers where they grow.' He then insisted that if I gave him two of my paintings he would feel well rewarded. He also suggested that I should spend the night in his house and not go to a hotel. Of course, I accepted, but I rather wondered what his guest room might be like.

After a very stimulating evening Raymond placed a camp bed for me in his all-purpose room and himself retired to the loft. As I got into bed an African brought in a glass tank in which were tropical fish. This he placed over a metal base containing glowing embers. Then he covered the whole thing with a blanket and left. It was not long before the smoke from the embers filled the room and nearly suffocated me, and I was torn between my long-ing to open the window and the certainty that this would kill the fish. Remembering Raymond's kindness to me when I was on the mountain I decided in favour of the fish but this meant a sleepless night for me.

Next morning I left the farm for Nairobi. When I reached it I found that my divorce had come through and George and I could now be married.

6

Exploring
the Northern Frontier
District

My first experience of what George's job involved shocked me and haunted me for a long time to come.

Rumours had reached the Game Department that some P.O.W.'s had disappeared from their barracks close to Nairobi; these overlooked the 'Lone Tree' plain. The area was teeming with game, which included a pride of eight lions. It was thought that the prisoners must have sneaked out hoping to add to their rations. What was certain was that they were never seen again. To prevent further tragedies George and a colleague were asked to shoot all the lions, if possible simultaneously. It was not an easy task. The pride needed to be located at a time when they were hungry. After studying the direction of the wind, bait was put out near a stream. Two cars were concealed nearby in the undergrowth. George wished me to wait in his car so that I could give help, if needed, and also to accustom me to the painful things that happened in a Game Warden's life and to which his wife must harden herself.

We waited for what seemed to me an eternity, then the first vultures spotted the bait and began to circle over the carcass, guiding the lions to it. Finally eight of them were tearing at it, cuffing and growling at each other to defend their meal. I had never been so close to even one lion before. The idea that within minutes all these splendid, golden cats would be dead, appalled me. Suddenly there was a volley of shots, lions were stumbling blindly in all directions in a wild effort to escape, only to collapse, whimpering almost like human beings. One of the pride got away, a lioness who was limping badly. George and his colleague went after her, while I remained sitting near to the bodies. Would I ever be able to harden myself to such gruesome control work? Even if it seemed justifiable to prevent those eight lions from developing into habitual man-eaters right on the outskirts of Nairobi – deep, deep inside myself I could not condemn that pride for having taken advantage of an opportunity provoked by people, who must have known that lions were on these plains.

When George returned after having shot the wounded lioness we transported the bodies to the Game Department and I needed all the self-control I could muster to keep my eyes on the road and not look at the people staring at our gruesome cargo.

After this grim experience we started off on the foot safari in the Mathews Range, which was to be our honeymoon. Only one white man besides George had explored this 100-mile-long mountain range. The local inhabitants were the Wandorobo, one of the two tribes indigenous to Kenya. Originally each family owned a mountain and guarded it by placing little wooden sticks along their footpaths. If a friendly visitor came to see the owners, he left similar sticks along his track. But if the owner found footmarks at other places, he knew that they belonged to a poacher or a honey thief. The latter were punished in a horribly cruel way – the tendons of their fingers were cut, then their crippled hands were tied into a ball with strong rope until they grew into useless stumps. After this the thief could only survive by gnawing at berries or by being fed by tribespeople who felt pity for him.

The Wandorobo lived in flimsy grass shelters which they left behind when they moved. We often found the glowing embers of a fire near such a hut which had been abandoned when its inhabitants heard us approaching,

After living in this undisturbed and wild area for several weeks, I well understood George's view that I would become so captivated by the Northern Frontier District that, even should our marriage prove a difficult one, I should never wish to leave it.

Having been used to an organised life, at first I found it difficult to adjust to a situation in which George would ask me to stock up with provisions for five weeks, only to find that our stay lasted six months, or to be told to get in food for three months and return in four weeks. However, I soon got used to going home with most of our provisions intact, or living off the land when they ran out.

While George dealt with poachers and other forms of game control I painted plants and collected them for the Nairobi Museum, for various international institutes, and for Kew Gardens. I had other occupations too: I excavated ancient sites, collected fossils, filled killing bottles with insects and preserved small reptiles and rodents.

Various dramatic incidents occurred. One day we heard the yapping of wild dogs and, following the sound through the forest, came upon a pack closing in on a Greater kudu which had fled to the very edge of a precipice. Panting heavily, the terrified animal faced certain death, either by plunging into the abyss, or by being torn to pieces by the pack. Trapped, he lunged bravely but hopelessly at the dogs. Instantly George fired, killing several of the pack whereupon the rest bolted and the kudu was saved.

On another occasion we found a baby Grevy's zebra that had been abandoned. We watched it for a very long time in case the mother should return. Eventually we took it home. It is always essential to observe the presumed orphan for a lengthy period before rescuing it because when the mother has to go away to feed, she always communicates to her young the need to stay put till she returns. The baby obeys this command literally. It can, therefore, easily happen that a young animal is picked up because it is believed to be abandoned, but in fact the mother later returns and the baby has been unnecessarily deprived of the freedom to live its natural life.

The little zebra was such an enchanting beast with its long legs, big head, woolly fur and reddish stripes, that I made several sketches of it which I still have today. We fed it on diluted Nestlé's milk and for some days it survived, then it died. Evidently the mother knew that it could not live and that was why she had left it, for animals obey the law of survival of the fittest.

Grevy's zebra are the handsomest of the species and the only ones that can be tamed. They are found in Kenya below an altitude of 3,000 feet. Between Nanyuki, a small township standing at 7,000 feet near the base of Mount Kenya and Isiolo, the altitude of which is 3,000 feet, there is a five-mile-wide area where the highland fauna changes to desert animals.

The N.F.D. is astonishingly rich in fauna including reticulated giraffe, blue-legged ostrich, oryx, Hunter's antelope, gerenuk and Grevy's zebra. These never cross to the highlands where wildebeest, pink-legged ostrich, Thomson's gazelle and Masaica giraffe occur. There are other species that co-exist throughout Kenya, they include hartebeest and Grant's gazelle, the pachyderms and predators.

The lion is found at various levels. In desert country up to 3,000 feet he is called *Felis somaliense* (after the Somalis living there). These lions are much smaller than those that live at higher altitudes. Often they have hardly any mane, they retain their spots almost indefinitely and can live for ten months without water, getting liquid from the blood of their prey and from roots and grasses.

Felis masaica lives mostly in Masai territory from 3,000 feet to 12,000 feet. He is less tough than *Felis somaliense*, in fact a lazy fellow with a splendid mane, who finds plenty of prey in his area but is very vulnerable because of his daily need of water.

The incident in which George killed the eight lions who were believed to have disposed of the human prisoners was one of many in which he was told to dispatch man-eaters. I have often been asked what turns a lion into a man-eater. There are a variety of causes: an old lion who has lost his teeth may find man the easiest prey, and the same could apply to a lion prevented from hunting by some injury. Then again, if African herdsmen sleep outside their thorn enclosure to avoid the noise and dust made by the livestock inside it, they offer a temptation to the lion since there is less risk in killing a man outside than in jumping inside the stockade to make a kill amongst the herd. As for the lions who kill wantonly and not for food, they appear to be as unusual and as abnormal as human mass murderers. But, if a pair of man-eaters have cubs, they teach their young similar habits.

The intelligence of lions is acknowledged and was demonstrated by a most extraordinary happening which took place when George was asked to kill two man-eaters. For the killing of man-eaters no methods are barred, so he put a small dose of strychnine into pieces of raw meat and placed these in the lions' latest pugmarks. They were soon taken. Observing this, George followed the lions' spoor; it led him to a bush covered with small red berries – *Cordia quarensis*. They are a violent emetic and Africans eat them when they wish to be sick. The lions had apparently laid up behind the bush, eaten the berries and vomited the whole contents of their stomachs, including the strychnine. Then they had walked off across rocks where it was impossible for George to track them. Though hardly credible, it appeared that when the lions felt ill they deliberately ate the berries, presumably knowing that they would make them vomit.

One thing I soon learned in my new life was never to go into the bush without a gun, for fear of surprising and frightening a sleeping animal, a sick one or a mother with her young. In such circumstances they would be most likely to charge. If so, a shot in the air would almost certainly turn them away.

In the past I had believed that so-called dangerous animals were fierce by nature and would attack any human being at sight, but the truth is they are peace-loving; all they ask is to be left alone and it is only when taken by surprise and feeling cornered that they become aggressive.

George wished me to gain practice in shooting, not just small animals for the pot, but also big game. After my experience with the buck at Seifenmühle I had intended never to kill again, and as the wife of a Game Warden I need not shoot for sport, but to assist George I had to become a good shot. My first kill was an elephant. Three had been raiding farmland near Isiolo and George had orders to dispose of them. I felt very sad when, backed by George in case I failed, I killed one of these splendid giants. He shot the other two; the local Turkana then had a feast of raw meat and it occurred to me that if I cooked part of the elephant's tongue for forty-eight hours in our pressure cooker, it might be palatable. I did this and when some unexpected guests arrived I dressed the tongue with herbs and announced it as a special

George Adamson, 1944

Joy on Mount Kenya,
during her flower
painting expedition

Lake Rudolf: Our landing bay at South Island

Daily encounters

Our 'bedroom'

Joy at work on one of her tribal paintings

treat. George took a mouthful and quickly left the room. I tried a bite and instantly joined him. The 'special treat' was as tough as rubber boots and the flavour was quite revolting.

Soon afterwards George received complaints about elephants raiding the maize fields at Wamba, a market centre for the Samburu tribesmen at the foot of the Mathews Range. To save time we sent the pack animals ahead and followed by car two days later. On our way we passed Archers Post; in 1900 this was the sole administrative station between Nairobi and Addis Ababa. Now a few foundation stones remained to mark the spot.

Around here the white limestone plain was barren and there was no sign of vegetation except for a few thorn trees and doum palms. We stopped at a spring which had been blasted into a small swimming pool by the army. The water was crystal clear for it was constantly absorbed by the limestone and constantly replenished by the spring. While enjoying a cool dip we found three-inch-long fishes of a species unknown to us. Later they were recognised as an unidentified type of tilapia. How they came to be in this pool, which was many miles from a river, remained a puzzle.

After we had crossed the plain the country became first hilly and then mountainous rising to an altitude of 8,000 feet. In the late afternoon we were driving below a high cliff when George pointed to black spots that were dotted all over it. As soon as he hooted, the black spots turned into baboons, who raced to the top of the cliff and disappeared. Evidently they had settled down for the night on the ledges, which to us were hardly visible, but which provided them with a leopard-proof dormitory.

When we reached Wamba we were sorry to hear from our herdsmen that two nights earlier a lion had jumped over the fence which was supposed to protect our pack animals and had killed one donkey and mauled three others so badly that they had all died. This had happened so quickly that the herdsmen had no time to save the animals, though one of them had eventually chased the lion with his spear.

We spent the night at Wamba because the local chief wanted George to shoot one of the marauding elephants and to leave the carcass where it fell to frighten the rest of the herd away. Elephants are known to be extremely sensitive to death, whether of their own kind or of human beings.

Before we had unpacked I was asked to buy a dwarf mongoose. This is Kipling's Riki Tiki Tavi and Wamba is famous for them. They live in large numbers in the nearby termite hills. It is unfortunate for these little clowns that they are both easy to catch and make endearing pets. As a result, many of them lose their freedom. Of course I bought this one and indeed, whenever I see a dwarf mongoose tied up in an African shop I buy it and release it in a suitable place.

It was a moonless night as we were led by local Africans to where the elephants were already in the maize. We followed the chief, trying to avoid breaking sticks or making any noise that might give our presence away. The stillness was absolute, although we knew the elephants were close there was no sound from them. The atmosphere was tense.

Suddenly the chief stopped and pointed to a dark mass. Because the prevailing wind had not carried our scent to them, we nearly collided with the herd. A single bull was only sixteen yards away from us. My job was to shine the torch to help George aim. I held it above his head, switched it on and focused. Two shots rang out and then two more, followed by a nerve-racking crash.

The stillness which followed the four shots was shattered by chatter and laughter and there were Samburu all around us, as though they had dropped from the sky.

Next morning we were woken by a noisy and rather irate group of tribesmen who begged us to shoot another elephant 'just to teach them'. George soon discovered the motive for their request. During the night three Wandorobo families had appeared and eaten all that was edible of the dead elephant so now the Samburu wanted to have a feast. In the circumstances George refused to kill another elephant.

That day we went towards Baragoi. We were crossing lion country and drove slowly ahead to protect the pack animals. Baragoi is a small village on the bank of a river that was now dry. On arrival we were told that a week earlier an elephant had killed a man and that since then it had returned daily at four in the afternoon to the scene of the tragedy (a further instance of the fascination which death seems to exercise over these animals). The local tribesmen wanted George to shoot the elephant and took us to the place where the man had been killed. There we saw a few tattered rags, deep holes where the elephant had rammed his tusks into the ground, and fresh spoor.

We tried to follow the tracks but saw only one peaceful elephant who quietly walked off when George put a few bullets over his head.

The inhabitants of Baragoi were in a poor way, for besides suffering from the effects of the recent drought, the neighbourhood had been devoured by a swarm of locusts which had left it looking like a desert. We gave the tribesmen all our water supply and left hurriedly, hoping to reach the next water-hole before nightfall.

By now, Pippin and the little mongoose had made friends so I rode on my mule, with the dog on my lap and the mongoose in my pocket. We reached the South Horr Valley before dark and came to a little stream. This valley is a paradise for elephants and other game which, in the dry season, congregate every evening at the water. By now we longed for a bathe but we knew we must wait till next morning for the elephants had 'right of water'.

We watched a baby elephant, certainly not more than a month old, who imitated all its mother's movements with the greatest concentration – flapping its ears, raising its trunk and making every effort to keep pace with her when she moved.

At dawn George sent off his game scouts to search for poachers. Most of all he wanted to capture the great Adukan, the chief of a large gang. Meanwhile we strolled along the dry river-bed till suddenly George pointed ahead and sank to the ground. I followed his example and saw a Lesser kudu. He was nibbling at the undergrowth while watching the moving shadows of the trees and listening for the slightest sound, such as the breaking of a twig. We were well concealed and up wind, which gave us a wonderful opportunity of watching this graceful and elusive antelope. It is one of nature's masterpieces, with its white lines crossing vertically down its silver-grey body, its half-moon-shaped white markings under its throat and white streaks on its face. Its head is crowned by lyre-shaped horns and its proportions are exquisitely balanced. Next to the reticulated giraffe the Lesser kudu is my favourite animal. Watching this one, until he sprang into the bush and vanished, we were entranced.

When we returned to camp we found a number of grim-looking poachers guarded by game scouts. While George was questioning them, two more scouts arrived, escorting an elderly Turkana – the great Adukan himself. He was a legendary figure and high rewards had been offered for his capture but always in vain. On one occasion, when a district officer was looking for him and passing along a narrow path at the foot of a cliff, Adukan had rolled a huge boulder down upon him. It missed by a few inches.

The game scouts when arresting Adukan had found plenty of evidence of his activities in the cave in which he had been caught. It was full of rhino horns, whips made of hippo skins, ivory earrings, and bracelets of giraffe hair and elephant tail-hair. All these Adukan had obviously intended to barter.

Now he stood before George stark naked and admitting all his crimes, with a broad grin. George asked him how he came to be caught. He explained that he had asked his 'oracle' about his future and had been told that he was going to be arrested. So, he put his things in order and just waited.

Telling the future by the 'oracle' is an old Turkana custom. It consists in throwing two sandals in the air, then observing the position in which they land and interpreting this. Impressed by Adukan's faith in his 'oracle', I asked him what was happening to my father. He sat down, threw the sandals and in a strange voice announced that my father was very well, was sending me lots of money and wished me good luck. Since my father had died so many years ago this only reinforced my scepticism about fortune-telling.

Very soon Adukan, though handcuffed, began ordering his fellow prisoners about; then, among the game scouts, he caught sight of some former members of his gang and presumably noticed that they looked fatter and happier than when they were working for him, and also that they respected and loved George. It was not long before he asked if he might join them, promising if he were accepted to lead the game scouts to hoards of ivory. George was familiar with this gambit and knew that most poachers enrolled on such a basis later ran away, but he trusted Adukan, took the risk and was justified. The old poacher remained for years with the game scouts, learned to use a rifle and when in action wore a high, red fez, apparently a symbol of his superiority. Now, as he was being marched away, we passed his camp and George asked him if he would like to visit his family. He declined with a grin, but suggested an advance on his future pay so that he could buy a goat for his people as a farewell present.

Next morning we saw deep below us Lake Rudolf looking like a blue mist surrounded by black lava. We now had to make our way across forbidding lava boulders to Teleki's Volcano. The donkeys had much difficulty in staggering across this wild country but at last we reached a wind-sheltered camp site. This was one of the spots where Count Teleki and Von Höhnel, who discovered Lake Rudolf and Lake Stefanie, had camped in 1888.

Pitching our tents was difficult as a strong gale tore the ropes out of our hands and filled our eyes and noses with sand. After a sleepless night we started off and soon came to a wide, sandy *lugga*; on the cliffs that bordered it I discovered rock engravings depicting mammoth giraffes, and antelopes with enormous horns. Louis Leakey had given me tracing material so I used it to record these remarkable pictures. Afterwards we rode on for three hours over old lava which was overlaid by more recent lava. I felt very uneasy if a lava blister sounded hollow under the mules' hooves. When at last we reached the base of Teleki's Volcano we tied our mounts to the few surviving *Boswellia carteri* trees, the species from which frankincense is produced. We then climbed to the rim of the crater.

When Lake Rudolf was first discovered this volcano was still active; since then three small volcanoes have erupted inside the crater floor. We had a fascinating view of the network of blue-black lava streams crossing the old lava and I drew a map indicating the latest eruptions. I thought it a pity I could not also record the smell coming from the many sulphur jets.

After this we made our way down to the lake, where Pippin

was waiting for us in the shade of a tree. It was midday and very, very hot. The lake looked tempting but we saw at least twenty crocodiles sleeping in the reeds, so we had to choose between riding for another three hours without shade to cool us or sharing the water with the crocs. We decided on the crocs. While one of us took a dip the other bombarded the beasts with stones. Nevertheless, one young croc followed us so persistently that in the end George was obliged to shoot him.

Refreshed, we went on to the Surima water-hole at the south of the lake, Pippin sitting on my lap to prevent his paws from being burned by the hot sand. We felt we had now earned a day's rest. I spent it exploring our immediate surroundings. A rock which overhung the Surima water-hole bore some engravings of camels and branding marks, all obviously recent. We asked some Rendile tribesmen who had carved them. They replied 'Bwana Reece'. Then about two miles inland I came across some very different rock carvings. At this point a gorge opened into a large circle, a spot which might have been used as a refuge or for meetings. Half-way up its steep walls was a narrow ledge and within a hand's reach above it, a number of rock engravings. One showed a long line of giraffes led by a man. I wondered if this might suggest that at the time the engravings were made giraffes were tame. There were also outline drawings of oryx, flamingoes, buffaloes, rhinos and some small antelopes. I traced them and afterwards, when I showed them to Louis Leakey, he was excited. Two years later they were reproduced by the journal of the National Historical Society of Kenya. Still later the originals were sent to England, where they aroused enough interest for a special meeting at Burlington House in London, because these were the first rock engravings found as far east in East Africa. Much later George and I saw similar engravings of mammoths in the caves of southern Spain, and in the Sahara Desert I also saw pictorial writings similar to the ones we found on Porr, a hill near to the El Molo Islands.

Our next visit was to the Hadado Springs. These are famous for the medicinal property of their water which is alleged to cure every ill, while the salt deposits around the springs are believed to make women fertile. Tribesmen came there from all over the area, as well as the Masai who live many hundred miles away. We sampled the water which had so strong a taste of sulphur that we spat it out but our pack animals delighted in it, indeed we found it difficult to drag them away from the springs.

We had brought a little flat-bottomed boat with us, hoping to cross over to South Island. This had only once been explored, that was in 1934 by an expedition led by Vivian Fuchs (later of Antarctic fame). His team had been overtaken by disaster and two of its members, Dyson and Martin, had been drowned. George had hoped to land on South Island during our safari but his plan, as it had been on his previous trips, was defeated by the notorious wind which made crossing impossible; this time it reached ninety-five miles an hour gale force.

Instead, we investigated the north-west side of the lake. We had to go mostly on foot as the lava-strewn ground was impossible for mules. The heat was intense and though we moved mostly by night I often plunged, fully dressed in jodhpurs, bush jumper and boots, into the lake so that I could cool down during the short time they took to dry. By day we had to cover every inch of our bodies to prevent our skin from being burned by the fierce sun and George even used lipstick to prevent his lips from cracking!

Amongst the lava we saw some emerald green grass which looked tempting to sit on, but when we did so we jumped up very rapidly as each blade was needle sharp. For the next weeks our wretched pack animals had little but this to eat, as a result many became ill and five donkeys died. Apart from the repellent grass there were a few puff-ball mushrooms. From these the Turkana crush a dark powder which they use for colouring their shields. One day, as I was passing a cliff of tuff I noticed fragments of pottery sticking out of it. These I collected and later sent to the Nairobi Museum. Their impressed markings were found to be of unknown origin.

We camped at Natron, a place where the rocky shore opens out into a deep lake. Here we were safe from crocodiles so we took our harpoon guns and our goggles and dived into the water. To our surprise we found two small, brightly coloured fish – one was red and, like a coral fish, had a 'false black eye' near its tail, and electric-blue and turquoise spots on the fins. The other looked as though it were made of black velvet, with iridescent blue spots on the fins. I sketched them from memory for I knew that once they were out of the water they would be bound to lose their colour. Later, having caught and killed them, we preserved them in salt and eventually sent them to the museum, where they were identified as a species so far known to be found only on the West coast of Africa. I also sent the museum a chameleon with white feet and white markings on its body, and a turtle which could deflate itself within its very flat shell. Both proved to be unknown species. While George fished I strolled along the shore, cutting out the fossilised bones of fish and large vertebrates from the rocks.

One afternoon, exhausted by the heat, I was resting in my tent when a long line of some hundred camels appeared over the hill. At every step they took, their hand-carved wooden bells gave a deep 'clonk, clonk'. Walking on the blue-black lava, with behind them the lead-coloured lake and above them the red evening sky, they looked more like a fairy-tale vision than reality. Moreover, the woman who led the caravan seemed to have stepped out of a fairy-tale. She was tall and long legged, with Mongolian features and her hair was built up into a coxcomb with red ochre and fat. From the waist down her body was covered in camel skins dyed in ochre, while her neck and shoulders were adorned with a wide collar made of strings of doum palm bark, richly interwoven with coloured beads. On her forehead three metal strings glittered and half-moon-shaped metal rings hung from her ears. Following her were a few good-looking Rendile men. These tribesmen are independent, truculent and wealthy.

Our next camp was at Loingalane, an oasis in this desert of lava. Here were springs of fresh water, soft grass and shade-giving doum palms. The coast of Lake Rudolf looked, from where we were, as though it were made of cotton wool, but when we moved towards it the whiteness took shape in flocks of pelicans, geese, ducks, ibis, spoonbills, flamingoes, storks, herons, gulls and other waterfowl. It was amusing to watch the pelicans fishing. They swam in open V-shaped formation, close behind each other, dipping their heads in unison into the water as they caught the fish which had swum into this V-shaped trap.

One day we paddled our dinghy over to the El Molo Islands. There we found several flimsy shelters made of a few sticks, covered with weeds taken from the lake – all were weighted down with boulders to prevent them from being blown away. These were the homes of two El Molo families. This tribe, which had been harassed by more virile people, at last found refuge on these little islands which, when Count Teleki discovered the lake, were still connected with the mainland.

The El Molo live on fish with occasional hippo or crocodile meat, or a turtle to make a change. From primitive rafts made of three doum palm trunks they fish using spears and nets, which are made of doum palm fibre, the only wood which does not rot in alkaline water. For plates the El Molo use turtle shells – and what precious plates these are, for the local turtle belongs to the *Trionyx* genus, which is only to be found in this lake and in the Nile. The British Museum had tried for many years to obtain such a turtle but without success. We, therefore, offered a large reward to anyone who could catch one for us with the result that it was not long before one was caught and presented to us. Later we sent it to London.

At the time the El Molo numbered only eighty persons, all of whom – owing to their highly alkaline diet and also to the frequency of incest – were very degenerate and suffered from scurvy and rickets. Nevertheless, they were most friendly and I was sad that they seemed doomed to extinction. Fortunately, this did not happen for the government learned of their plight and provided them with sheep, goats and vegetables.

I wanted to paint an El Molo couple, I didn't mind which, for to me they all looked exactly alike. George offered tobacco as a reward to the models and they queued up to sit for me. In spite of their extreme poverty these kindly people offered us piles of giant tilapia, which are very good eating. When George shot a croc they became most excited and fought for the flesh, they also grabbed at the tough skin which they assured us was equally delicious. One evening we searched round our tent for crocs. Their eyes were reflected in the light of our torch. George shot eleven after which we thought the others would surely go away, so what was my horror when I woke up next morning to see one in front of my tent! I shot it from my bed.

George now concentrated on the local poachers and I explored another of the islands. On a little plateau I saw several cairns. I asked our staff to remove the stones. At its base was a large slab and beneath it sand and a few bones. I had learned in Zurich, and from the Leakeys, never to pull out a bone but to brush away the sand until connected bones were exposed. Here I found a complete skeleton; it had been buried in a crouching position, turned to the right and with its hands and knees close to the face. I photographed it and sketched it all carefully; I then wrapped the bones in cotton wool and placed them in a box. In a second grave I discovered a similar skeleton. Close to the graves I found a yellow portulaca, the first flower I had seen near Lake Rudolf. Later it was identified as a new species.

After this we approached Mount Kulal, a twenty-eight-mile-long volcanic range running parallel to the lake, about twenty miles to the north of it. When its volcano ceased to be active an earthquake split the range at its centre. The result was a circular abyss 4,000 feet in depth and four miles wide. The walls then split into sections resembling the segments of an opened orange, connected at the base but fanning out at the top. All along the range were very steep, narrow ridges. They led to the top which was covered with rain-forest. From the plains Kulal looked like an insignificant hill but it is in fact one of the world's wonders; almost the equal of the Grand Canyon of Arizona.

We reached the base of the range at sunset and the men set to work to make a *boma* to protect our pack animals. While this was going on, local tribesmen told us that some lions had been harassing the camels of the few Rendile and Samburu who live near the summit. They asked George to shoot them. He was surprised as he had never heard of lions on Kulal, only of buffalo and Greater kudu. In the past there had also been elephants but these had been exterminated long ago by poachers. Next morning we tried to find a ridge wide enough for the donkeys to clamber up but in the end we had to unload them and carry their packs in the many places where it was too narrow for them to pass.

After we had climbed nearly 5,000 feet we reached the summit. The intense heat had changed to ice-cold and we sat in the dripping rain-forest by a fire, wearing thick pullovers and looking through a curtain of grey lichen at the shimmering heat of the lake far below.

Next morning while George interrogated poachers, I took my sketch book and watercolours and went with a guide to the central abyss, the rim of which was so narrow that in some places we had to slide along it with our legs dangling over each side. The view was panoramic and to convey its awe-inspiring grandeur I had to take three sheets of paper and sketch it in sections.

The following morning we went down into the immense desert in order to explore the gorge which led to the central abyss. As we walked along the narrow track, flanked by sheer walls 100 yards high and often so close to each other that we could barely stretch out our arms sideways, we met two rhinos who obviously lived there. Fortunately, we were able to jump up on to a narrow ledge covered with bush and so avoid being charged. Later we came to a huge boulder with a deep rain pool in front of it; this made further progress impossible. We had walked about two miles but were still far from the centre of the abyss. We now turned back and then climbed the southern face of Kulal. The track was very narrow but it was just possible for the donkeys to pass. Suddenly, they all panicked and on the next ridge we saw a rhino running downhill like a tank out of control. It was separated from us by a deep valley but all the same it was a very frightening sight. That night we pitched our camp on the southern summit, which was as cold and misty as the northern summit.

Suddenly a few Samburu elders appeared and begged George to shoot a lion that had been killing their cattle. We were told that the lion made a habit of hiding on the branch of a tree, watching the cattle pass by and then when he had selected his victim, springing upon it and dragging it away while the rest of the herd bolted. We were shown deep scratches on the trunk of a tree, which appeared to have been made by a lion and convinced us of the truth of the story. While our staff set up camp and made a very strong *boma* for the donkeys we went in search of the lion and sighted him not far away. He was obviously interested in our donkeys, but vanished before George could shoot. Throughout the evening we were on the alert; then, about 10 p.m., George grabbed his rifle and fired two shots. Three lions had jumped over the thorny fence and one of our donkeys had been badly mauled. George had killed one lion and wounded another, the third had escaped. It was astonishing that none of the pack animals had made any noise when the lions attacked them. Unfortunately, the donkey's wounds went septic and he died. We tried to follow the spoor of the lion but there were so many cattle tracks that we were unable to trace it.

Next morning a baby buffalo joined our safari, he had lost his mother. Some Samburu brought him in and asked us to look after him. They also brought a good supply of milk; he took easily to a bottle and feeding him was no problem. He was still furry and had outrageously large ears with long hair on their ends. I called him 'Segeria Egitoki' which means 'Long Ears' in Samburu. We thought he must be about two weeks old and assumed that his mother had been shot by poachers. Small as Egitoki was, he was already strong enough to toss an unwary person, and if one of our staff bent down the little buffalo would put his head between the man's legs and send him head over heels.

There were already two tiny knobs on Egitoki's forehead, later they would develop into formidable weapons but at the moment he was an affectionate, if boisterous, baby who sucked my thumb and followed us about wherever we went. Feeding him, however, became a problem as he needed four bottles of milk a day. Besides, we had to continue our safari into the desert and he was used to a cool climate, also he would be unable to walk such a distance at our pace. We, therefore, hired a cow in milk and her calf, and also two camels. We then made a pannier out of sticks padded with grass and tied it to one of the camels. In this cradle Egitoki was carried 100 miles across the desert to where our lorry was waiting. The little caravan consisted of the leading camel, whose tail was tied to the second camel which carried Egitoki, then came the cow and her calf, followed by a string of prisoners guarded by game scouts.

When we reached Baragoi, Egitoki was in excellent shape and had become everyone's pet. The prisoners, who had probably killed his mother, were delighted with him. Indeed, we were all sorry when he went off to Hook's farm where Raymond hoped to cross him with cows.

7

The Congo Again

When in 1944 George was due for some leave, we decided to visit the Congo. The authorities of the Kenya National Parks gave us an introduction to their opposite numbers in the Belgian Congo National Parks and asked that we should be allowed to climb the still active volcanoes. Of these there are seven and they erupt in a cycle of seven years; in 1944 it was the turn of Nyiragongo which is close to Lake Kivu.

We took the route Sally Atsatt and I had taken earlier and at last we came in Ruanda Urundi to the base of the extinct volcano Muhavura. We knew that this volcano was one of the homes of the mountain gorillas and, hoping to see them, hired a guide to lead us up the thickly forested slopes to the summit. We had a 13,000-foot climb before us and as we advanced the going got steeper and steeper. In places it was like climbing a staircase. We saw a few spoor and some fresh droppings of gorillas but they had obviously got our wind and fled. Hour after hour we struggled upwards till the vegetation thinned out and we had a vast view of the countryside below us. The weather was overcast and our guide urged us to hurry if we wanted to reach the summit before mist made further progress impossible. Already there was a slight drizzle. This was tantalising for there were many plants new to me and I would have liked to examine them. We had just reached the top and seen a deep crater lake when thick fog came down, making it urgent for us to hurry back if we were to avoid getting lost. The descent was much more taxing than the ascent; our knees became wobbly and every step was a hazard, as well as an effort. When we had reached camp I asked our guide to take us up one of the other two volcanoes next day. Smiling he shook his head and said we had better wait a little. How right he was we realised the following morning when we found we could hardly walk a step, and that even driving was painful.

We felt, however, just fit enough to visit the Watusi, a giant race. As we approached their settlement we saw several healthy-looking men, holding parasols, sitting upright on litters that were being carried by porters. When we made enquiries we were told that these men were nobles and that the nobility never walked. Next we passed some round huts, white-washed and beautifully decorated with designs carried out in red ochre and black ash. The people, we noticed, carried hand-woven baskets of exquisite shapes.

Later we saw more elaborate huts and finally came to the King's Palace. We had an introduction to him from the Kenyan authorities and next day were ushered into his presence.

King Mwani Charles Mutura Rudahigwa was so tall that I found it a strain to hold my head high enough to be able to look him in the eyes. In his beautifully proportioned reception room we talked about the history of the Watusis and also discussed their famous long-haired cattle. These came from the Balkans; they were never milked and, of course, never slaughtered. It seemed that this status was similar to that of the holy cows of India. Mwani Charles spoke English and French fluently and was dressed like any European Head of State. He had just returned from an official visit to Belgium. In my ignorance of Watusi etiquette I asked if I could paint a portrait of him. With a charming smile he replied that it would be difficult for him to find the time. He did, however, consent to my taking a photograph. Encouraged by this, I asked if I might also photograph Her Majesty, his mother, but he explained that she lived in a palace some distance away. Persisting in my enquiries I asked if I might photograph the famous cattle but was told that they were grazing on a far mountain so that they might be in splendid condition for a special ceremony a little later.

No doubt I looked disappointed so the king kindly asked his A.D.C. to organise a warriors' dance on the following day. They gave a splendid performance, the tall, graceful men leaping high up in rhythmic movements. But alas much of their traditional garb had been replaced by modern substitutes – for instance, multi-coloured strips of cotton now fell from their waists to the ankles, replacing the original draperies. Only the knee-high drums to which they danced were genuine.

Our next stop was at Lake Kivu where we called on the District Officer who supplied us with an escort. The roads around the lake were blocked in some places by lava flows and there were many dangerous hairpin bends.

Wherever we went the silhouette of Nyiragongo haunted us and when, after dark, we watched the red clouds rise at short intervals from the boiling lava cascading down the slopes of the volcano, the sight was breathtaking. For the next lap of our journey the National Park authorities provided us with a guide and porters to help us in our climb up the mountain. They advised us to camp some 100 yards below the crater rim because of the poisonous sulphur fumes.

On our way up through the rain-forest I saw many plants that did not grow in Kenya. Of course I knew that it was strictly forbidden to pick any flowers inside a National Park but I could not resist taking and sketching a ruby-red Epiphitic Orchid (*Polystachya kermesina*) and a *Begonia wollastonii*. In doing so I felt doubly guilty because not only was I breaking the rules but on top of this I was the guest of the Director, Dr De Wilde. I assuaged my conscience with the thought that my sketches might be of some value to botanists. On our return I confessed my crime, upon which I was told politely, but firmly, that my sketches would be confiscated and sent to Antwerp and that I could expect further repercussions. There were no repercussions for several years, then I received the third volume of *Spermatophytes en Flore du Congo Belge* published by the Institut des Parcs. In it I saw my sketches used as a coloured frontispiece and with the book came a grateful note from the Director, saying what a very valuable contribution they had made to this luxury edition.

It was late in the afternoon when we reached a suitable camp site near the top of the volcano. From there we walked to the crater rim. The wind was blowing the fumes in the opposite direction so we were able to have a clear view. The central wall of the crater fell 600 perpendicular feet to a flat floor which had a circular opening in its centre. From this rose dark-red fumes which condensed into thick billowing clouds that exploded high up in the air. We were deafened by the raging of the magma boiling deep below us.

The spectacle was overpowering and George and I sat in utter silence as the light faded and the pulsating fire clouds rose above us into a black infinity. I had the impression that I was witnessing something that man was not intended to see: nature's never-resting force shaping our planet – one of so many planets much larger than Earth. How insignificant it made human beings seem.

Later we visited another volcano, Nyamlagira. This was the one that Sally Atsatt and I had watched some years ago pouring lava into the lake. Now the vast crater had cooled down and we were given permission to walk across it, at our own risk. We found that the main crater included several smaller craters, each at a different stage of cooling and all connected by a mass of lava of different formations. Piled-up fragments, with knife-sharp edges towered over beds of pumice; rough boulders pressed between pinnacles that emerged like sentinels through concertina-shaped lava streams from which sulphur-smelling jets hissed.

The ground beneath my feet often sounded frighteningly hollow and I feared that the crust would break under my weight and precipitate me into the boiling cauldron.

Our expedition was certainly risky, possibly foolish, but we felt an indescribable urge to look into a world that was normally denied us. I was terrified by being totally cut off from organic life and yet I felt more strongly than ever before a conviction that nearness to death gives rise to spiritual awareness.

In spite of the magnificence of the volcanoes, we had never given up hope of seeing the forest gorillas and so, when we neared Lubero, in which area these apes are to be found, we called on the Game Warden and asked his permission to search for them. Gorillas are very highly protected and it was only because George, as a colleague, was trusted that he agreed to our request. He was very helpful for, since our time was short and the forests where the gorillas live are very dense, he sent some scouts out to locate a troop. When they returned, we set off.

Walking in silence, in single file, accompanied by thirty beaters, we scrambled over fallen trees and got entangled in lianas as we crawled up and down the steep slopes. At times we caught the very strong scent of gorillas and observed their excrement, which was as thick as my arm. On several occasions our guide nearly collided with the leader of a troop, who had evidently waited in the hope of frightening us away by a charge. Unlike other primates whose leading female has the task of protecting the group, in the case of gorillas it is the oldest male who guards his family by staying at the rear and facing the danger. We had only a fleeting glimpse of two females crossing a forest glade; each was holding her baby at her breast and both were jumping on three legs.

Feeling weary after our long stalk, we sat down and listened to alarming stories about dangerous gorillas told us by the beaters, some of whom even showed us scars to prove the veracity of their tales. Perhaps the leading gorilla was listening for suddenly he emerged from a thicket, let out a piercing cry and made straight for us. Luckily he stumbled over a branch and fell, giving us time to jump to our feet, at which he vanished. Our guide then told us that we had better go home for if we further provoked that gorilla he might well charge in earnest. We took his advice.

We had had eight sightings of gorillas, which was a good score, many people had searched for days and never caught a glimpse of them.

George had always wanted to visit Gangala Na Bodio, the place where African elephants are trained to work. The experiment was initiated by King Albert of Belgium at a time when it was planned to open a part of the Congo which was inaccessible to mechanical transport. In India, the more docile and smaller elephants have long been taught to cooperate with man. There an elephant of about four years old is isolated from the herd and then roped. Escorted by two already tamed elephants, it is led to the training station and placed in a paddock. When it is time to teach the elephant to lie down, a padded wooden block is released from above him and lightly pressed on to his shoulders. This first step towards obedience is usually achieved within four days and with no harmful side effects.

Unfortunately, the African elephant, a much stronger creature and more obstinate, proved far more difficult to train. In order to make him lie down a chain was secured to each of his feet, which were gradually forced apart till they could not support his weight so that the poor beast collapsed. Later, these elephants obeyed the slightest touch or order of their mahout. There had, however, been a few fatal accidents, even among men who had worked with the elephants for many years. Is one to attribute this to the unpredictable nature of a wild elephant, or to the old adage that 'an elephant never forgets'? Whatever the truth may be my sympathy goes to the elephant for I do not believe that anything constructive can be achieved by force.

Captain Flieshower, the senior Game Warden of the Congo, was against the training of elephants in present circumstances. He pointed out that there were now tractors which could bulldoze twenty-four hours a day, could penetrate the thickest jungle and that, even if they were expensive to run this was nothing compared to the cost of keeping elephants. Besides, elephants could only work for four consecutive hours, for the remainder of the day they needed to feed, to sleep and to be taken to the river – a daily bath was essential if they were to remain in good condition because their skin needed to be kept moist. Finally, elephants cannot be moved from one region to another as, apart from the question of transport, they become acclimatised to one area and often fall ill if taken elsewhere.

Captain Flieshower asked us if we thought that trained elephants might be taken on by the Kenyan authorities as a tourist attraction. But George, knowing that the policy of the National Parks was to leave the animals in their wild state, did not offer much hope.

We were lucky to be shown the quarantine quarters of the okapi. These rare and beautiful animals are the giraffe's nearest relations. While in quarantine they were kept isolated from each other till it was certain that they were free from infection and could be sent to zoos, where they would be amongst the most expensive exhibits. Okapis were very difficult to rear until it was discovered that the fatal infection they so often develop in captivity comes from a parasite which lives in their excrement. Of course, in the wild, they would rarely, if ever, step into their excrement and this explains why the infection is chiefly found among captive animals. Once the parasite had been identified and was known to be the cause of the disease, a cure was quickly found.

On our return journey we reached Beni at Christmas time and decided to visit the Hoyo Caves, which were only a few hours' drive away. We brought some drinks and delicacies with which to celebrate the festive season and set off down a track which led to the forest. It had not been used for a long time and was now so rough that the Land-Rover could hardly advance along it. We had just decided that we must turn back when we were confronted by a beautiful rose garden and at its far end, a white house with a thatched roof, from which emerged an attractive young blonde in the shortest of shorts and a much older man. They were as surprised to see us as we were to see them. After we had introduced ourselves they invited us to spend Christmas with them.

Mr Ruthcart had been for many years the senior geologist in the Belgian Congo and it was he who discovered the Hoyo Caves. He had hoped that they would be explored immediately but there never seemed to be enough money to mount an expedition, so it was not until he had retired that he had an opportunity to investigate them. He found that there were seven caves yielding rich guano deposits and also fossils of extinct animals.

When the Belgian Government learned of these valuable discoveries, they provided money to explore the caves, but unfortunately, the outbreak of the Second World War put an end to these activities.

Mr Ruthcart gave us a fascinating description of the caves which were almost inaccessible, the entrances to most of them being high above the present ground level and well concealed. He had been obliged to use long ladders to reach the openings which were so narrow that he had much difficulty in squeezing himself through.

Inside were enormous vaults, mostly covered with guano. During later explorations he found a lake and several waterfalls; the caves were on different levels and led for distances, as yet unknown, into the range of the Great Rift.

After digging cross-sections into the guano to be able to estimate its depth, fossils of extinct fauna were exposed. Mr Ruthcart sent some samples to Antwerp, where they aroused great interest. How these animals had entered the caves is likely to remain a mystery until more is known about the movement and folding of the strata of the Great Rift.

We were taken to visit two of the caves; they had now been lit by electricity, so we were able to see the vast labyrinth of gorges and tunnels, while in the distance we heard the thunder of a waterfall. Whether, since the tragic civil war in the Congo, these caves have been explored and exploited we long to know.

Oma died peacefully at Seifenmühle on 17 April 1946. Her coffin was carried on a farm wagon to the cemetery. By then our family had been entirely dispossessed.

Traute and my mother remained in Vienna, Dorle settled in England and the others were scattered around the world. Finally, the valley of the Seifenmühle was drowned by the largest reservoir in Czechoslovakia; with it went most of my happiest memories. I have never gone back to the district for I wish to keep my early recollections of the beauty of Seifenmühle intact.

I now received a number of commissions to paint flowers and also sold some of my previous paintings to the museum.

Our next safari took us to Kolbio on the Somali border. Here George became so ill with dysentery that he could not even sit up, so I drove him, as fast as I could, to Malindi on the coast, where the nearest doctor lived.

He soon recovered but still needed rest, so we decided to accept an invitation to stay on and celebrate the end of the fast of Ramadan. I was so impressed by the splendour of the traditional robes worn by the Arabs on this occasion that I asked the District Officer whether he could induce one to sit for me. I had so far had no experience in portrait painting and I was, therefore, most embarrassed when next day the *Liwali*, Sheikh Azan appeared. He was a very much respected and important person for he was the religious leader as well as the chief judge of the Arab community that lived on the coast. I was further alarmed when he told me that he had recently been painted by a well-known French artist. I wondered whether to confess how little I knew about portrait painting. I did not do so but the Patriarch did not take long to size up the situation and realised that I was totally inexperienced. However, being the epitome of a gentleman he sat through his ordeal without complaint. The result of my efforts was no masterpiece but I have kept this sketch till today. Little did I then imagine that it was to be the forerunner of 700 portraits of Kenyan tribesmen wearing their traditional ornaments, and that I would spend six years in remote places making these records.

From Malindi George and I went by lorry to the Boni Forest. This is parkland about 30 miles wide, running parallel to the coast from Lamu to the Somali border. We had to cut a track through this swampy area which was rich in game and poaching was rife. George had to deal with offenders; then we went on to Kiunga, a tiny fishing village by the sea, and within a few miles of the border. The day after we arrived heavy rain fell and we were marooned for several weeks. Luckily we had brought harpoon-guns and goggles, so we were able to explore many coral gardens where I saw a greater variety of those 'fairy-tale' fish than I had seen at Port Sudan. Knowing that when taken out of the water they lose their iridescence within minutes, I took my paint-box to the reef and, putting the freshly caught fish in a basin, I made a quick colour sketch. Later, on the shore, I made a detailed water-colour drawing from my sketches and in this way achieved an authentic record. Then I preserved the fish in salt and later took them to the Nairobi Museum where plaster-casts were made of them.

The Mombasa Municipality bought eighty of these paintings, intending to exhibit them in the future Marine Museum. Alas, by the time it opened, most of my pictures had been stolen, and thus the only record of coral fish painted on the reef was lost.

At this time I was ill and unhappy and eventually decided to go to London for treatment. While there I hoped to occupy my evenings carving ivory chess-men. The pawns were to depict African boys and girls, the kings and queens would be Africans wearing spectacular head-dresses, giraffes would be the knights and phallic totems the castles.

We bought ivory chips from the Game Department and I sawed them into blocks of three different sizes. Until I got my passage I spent my time painting portraits of the tribesmen I met on my safaris, with the intention of using them as models for the chess-men.

On my voyage to England I met a fellow passenger who was interested in Africans living in remote places and I showed him my sketches. He suggested that when I arrived I should show them to Michael Huxley, editor of the British *Geographical Magazine*. To my surprise, he invited me to write an article to be illustrated by my sketches. Since I had little experience in writing, I suggested that Alys Reece should supply the text. Later, our joint effort appeared in the magazine.

While in England I was invited to stay with Susi Jeans and her husband, Sir James. Susi had been an old friend and contemporary in my Vienna days. She was a brilliant musician who played the organ and had given concerts in Vienna, Paris and London. Sir James, too, played the organ and found relaxation in music from his studies in mathematics, physics and astronomy.

There was a difference of thirty years between Susi and James but their marriage was a very happy one, they had three small children and lived in a big house at Box Hill which stood in some thirty acres of ground. Although Susi and I had married in the same month, I had never met her husband. Now, having read some of his books, I felt in awe of him. At breakfast on the first morning after my arrival he told me a lot about Box Hill – that it was on a mediaeval pilgrims' highway and that during the Second World War it was believed to be directly on the route by which the Germans meant to invade England. The house had been occupied by the Ministry of Defence and James had only recently returned to it. Now, of course, there were no staff but the great scientist cheerfully helped his wife and me wash up the breakfast dishes and later assisted in other household chores.

In the afternoon we listened to Susi practising for her next recital on the only copy of the organ at Leipzig on which Bach had played. James had had it made for her. Now, his face flooded with happiness, he stood behind her watching her as she played Scarlatti. Later, many of the Jeans' friends arrived; each played his own instrument, whether harpsichord, clavichord or piano. It was a most stimulating afternoon.

When their guests had left Susi went upstairs to put the children to bed and I stayed talking to James, who was leaning against the organ. Suddenly his face grew very pale and his breathing became laboured. I suggested that he should loosen his collar, helped him to a chair and rushed off to fetch Susi. I had been told that James suffered from angina and that when he had had previous attacks Susi had given him injections. This time she arrived too late. He died as she entered the room. Neither she nor I had ever before been so close to death.

During the next few hours James's face was transformed by a sort of spiritual radiance which I felt, far more than his books, expressed his genius. In Africa I had often seen dead animals or their skeletons on the sun-parched plains and had accepted the fact that death was a recycling of organic matter. But now, seeing the way in which it could purify the physical shell of a great mind, I felt I had come nearer to understanding the spiritualising quality of the transition from life to death.

So impressed was I that I suggested to Susi that a death mask should be made. It now lies in her music room.

A few weeks later I moved to London and took a room close to the psycho-analyst who was treating me. I spent a lot of time visiting picture galleries, trying unsuccessfully to understand surrealist art. Hoping that a contemporary of Augustus John and Bernard Shaw might help me I called on Dame Ethel Walker who, old and frail, was then living in one room in Chelsea. Its walls were covered with her superb paintings. When I asked her what she intended to do with them, she shrugged her shoulders and said she might well leave them to the girl who cleaned the place. Dame Ethel, though very poor, did not wish to part with a single one of her paintings during her lifetime. After her death several were acquired by the Tate Gallery. She invited me to visit her again and, when I did so, introduced me to the Director of the Slade. Having looked at my sketches of African tribesmen and heard for how short a time I was going to be in England and how much I wanted to attend the Slade, he allowed me to cut the queue.

I did not enjoy making pencil sketches of the capitals of ancient pillars so, after a time, I took my easel and walked boldly into the life class to join the most advanced students. I was amazed that I got away with this infiltration since it must have been evident to all that I was a beginner. But I was accepted and made consider-able progress.

When I left London I stopped at Zurich on my way to Vienna. There I called on Dr Walter Robert Corti, the Director of the magazine *Du*, who wanted to see some of my flower pictures to illustrate an article on Kenya. I spent an interesting evening with him during which he told me of his belief that wars should not be fought and that by breaking down hate and prejudice between people of different nations it should be possible to build a cosmo-politan generation. He intended to bring up orphaned children whose parents had been killed fighting on opposite sides and educate them together until they were old enough to choose their careers. The Swiss Government supported his experiment and other countries too were cooperating. To give his young students the opportunity of handling objects from other con-tinents and thereby widening their interests, he asked me to send him things such as shells, porcupine quills or even artifacts such as little toys made by African children. I was of course delighted to send him gifts which would be stimulating to the recipients and received an ample reward in the grateful letters that came to me from the children.

At this time Vienna was still occupied by the Allied Forces – England, France and Russia – and it was very difficult to get permission to enter it. However, after skiing for several weeks near Innsbruck and calling repeatedly at the British Embassy I obtained a pass to visit my family for two weeks. I went by train to Vienna, travelling second class. I had the whole com-partment to myself, so I offered seats to some elderly Austrians, standing cramped in the corridor outside.

By an extraordinary coincidence two old friends of mine were amongst them – both had wanted to marry me, some fifteen years ago. Nice they were, but I was glad I had refused their proposals, now we had even less in common than fifteen years earlier.

At the station Traute and a few friends awaited me with flowers. We went straight to the top of the spire of St Stephen's Cathedral, I had never been up there before. Poor Vienna. I nearly cried when I saw the inner city shattered by bombs, debris blocking the streets and many of the landmarks gone.

We then drove to see my mother, who looked very aged and thin and was wearing a dress which I remembered from fifteen years back. We took her on a tour of the city. Several of Vienna's famous squares now harboured statues of Stalin and Lenin – they had replaced those of the Habsburgs. One day my mother and I went to the Prater to sketch one of its magnificent trees, but we had to give up our plan when two Russian soldiers appeared with obvious intentions. I thundered at them in English and they bolted, but we thought it best to go home.

My mother told me of the rapings and other brutalities suffered by the women of Vienna since it had been occupied by Russian troops. Many Viennese lived on the Black Market to supplement the meagre rations, with the result that corruption was replacing the charm of pre-war Vienna. When my permit expired I returned to Kenya very depressed.

8

Painting Safaris

George met me at Nairobi and we went to the farm which he and his brother Terence had inherited; it was a stone house standing in 100 acres of coffee plantation. When I arrived I found Pippin chained to a table. His appearance shocked me very much. He dragged himself along to greet me, all his gaiety gone – it took weeks for him to become his former self and he never again sang duets with me.

The farm was at Limuru, sixteen miles from Nairobi, in much too suburban an area to please George and Terence. They were not sorry to part with it when the government eventually requisitioned the place, but were paid only a nominal sum by way of compensation.

Knowing how much I loved safaris George now concentrated on his control work in the remote northern area of the N.F.D. We were alone for long periods and once spent eight whole months without seeing a single European. I painted and collected insects, fossils, small reptiles and rodents for the Nairobi Museum and also supplied the Entomological Department with various unknown species of moths. These I caught by placing a basin of water outside our tent after dark, and into it a lamp. This had the advantage of the light attracting every moth in the area, which then fell into the water for me to collect – as well as keeping our tent free of them.

One of the facts I learned at this time was how rhinos, in waterless regions, get the salt they need. Near Marsabit we found a cave that had been excavated and saw that its walls were scratched as high as the rhinos' horns would reach as they licked the saline rock.

Meanwhile, George was dealing with poachers, settling tribal fights about water-holes and helping to control anthrax, rinder-pest and foot-and-mouth disease.

He was the one member of the Game Department who had his own mules and donkeys and these he had trained for long safaris. It was partly thanks to them that I was able to accompany him. As the only woman travelling in the most distant areas of the N.F.D. I was often asked whether I did not miss social life and home comforts. In fact our nomadic existence was full of enormous interest and provided me with so many compensations that I had little time for feeling lonely. However, there was one thing I did miss – music. In Isiolo there was my small piano, treated to withstand the tropical climate; I had bought it with money I had made by selling my paintings. I also missed a relaxing soak in a hot bath, for which standing on one leg in a small canvas tub was a very poor substitute.

We seemed to be always on the move for either we ran out of provisions, or George collected so many poachers that he had to take his prisoners back to Isiolo. During our short stays there we kept open house, which was not easy as we had very little money because members of the Game Department were paid the lowest salaries of all Government employees, and this even though their department provided the highest revenues. However small our budget we entertained people from all walks of life. Amongst our visitors were scientists, hunters, and film producers who needed George's advice about where to find wild animals. One film company wanted to stage an elephant stampede, but without upsetting the animals too much. George gave them a dry lion skin from his control storage and told them to wave it at the elephants. This did the trick.

There was an amusing incident one morning when three scruffy looking men peeped into the sitting room, as though they were expected. I was still in my dressing-gown, waiting for George to come to breakfast. (He usually spent an hour in his office before doing so.) So I told the men that this was a private house and if they wanted to see my husband they should go to the office. At that moment George appeared, looking rather peevish, and introduced the United States' Attorney-General and two of his colleagues whom he had invited for breakfast.

Those we liked we invited for a meal and many 'calls' expected to last for a few hours ended by stretching into weeks as our guests decided to join our safaris. I always kept a few wooden camel bells and other small gifts, the sort of things that our new friends could not buy in souvenir shops and on the other hand could accept without feeling under any obligation. We made many friends – our acquaintances fell roughly into two categories: those who had become so dependent on the rigid controls which business and social life had inflicted on them that they could not adapt to the improvisations and sudden changes which a life close to nature demands; in consequence they wanted to return as quickly as possible to the safety of their fireplaces. The other group represented the opposite extreme – all their lives they had been frustrated, so now they became almost drunk with their sudden freedom, and shedding their inhibitions really enjoyed themselves. I sympathised with both groups, though I preferred the 'let's go wild' group.

About this time we had to move from the Government-owned house where we had been living, to a new HQ which was only three miles from the administrative centre. Because funds were so low George and his brother Terence offered to help build the house. It was such a success that Terence was then offered a Government job in the building department. This he refused.

Our new home, built of local stone, nestled in hills that formed a large horseshoe. From it we overlooked the vast plains to the north of Isiolo. It was spacious enough for our needs, though our guests had to be satisfied with tents.

In March 1948 George had to go north to the Ethiopian border to put a stop to raids around important water-holes. It was thought that this operation might give rise to a tribal war so I was not allowed to go with him. To fill in time I joined a Swedish expedition which had just arrived in Kenya, intending to study the flora and fauna of the high mountains of East Africa, Ruanda Urundi and the Belgian Congo.

Having painted some of the flora of Mount Kenya and of Kilimanjaro, I was anxious to record that of Ruwenzori and Mount Elgon.

The leader of the expedition was Dr Ake Holm, a world authority on spiders; the botanist was Dr Olaf Hedberg; both were from the University of Uppsala, other members came from various parts of Sweden. Ruwenzori lies half in Uganda and half in the Congo. It was difficult at this time to get permission to make the climb from the easier Congo level so we were obliged to hire porters and cut our way up the very steep, forested slope on the Ugandan side.

While waiting for the porters to be equipped and organised, I became fascinated by some Pygmies who were living temporarily amongst the Bantus here, and I painted a man and a woman. I was puzzled by the fact that the woman wore a metal necklace which was identical with those I had seen Gabra women wearing, but the Gabra were of Hamitic stock, and lived hundreds of miles away. The Wakamba women, who were Bantus and lived close to Nairobi, also had similar necklaces. I wondered whether this could be evidence of some long-forgotten migration of these people, during which they might have exchanged or copied each others' ornaments.

Ruwenzori has a reputation for heavy rain falling for 365 days in the year. We soon had evidence to support the statement. During our ascent not only had we to walk through icy rivers that came down from the snow-line, but day after day we were drenched. We felt particularly sorry for the porters who had heavy enough loads to carry even when these were not waterlogged. The higher we climbed, the more sponge-like was the moss that covered the ground – while the trees, their branches covered with moss and with lichen hanging between them, looked rather like green teddy bears.

When we reached the moorland our progress was still slower, for high tussocks were the only solid ground in the midst of a swamp and we had to jump from one to another if we did not wish to end up in a smelly morass. The poor porters, with their soggy loads, had a tough time and I was thankful that I had left Pippin with friends.

We pitched our camp in the 'Bigo' moorland, from where we could see the shimmering glaciers on four of the six mountains which form the Ruwenzori range. Luckily, from now onwards the weather cleared and we were able to botanise amongst the giant lobelias and senecios which grew next to the blue ice.

The highest of the Ruwenzori peaks is 16,794 feet but proved easier to climb than Mount Kenya. To his delight Ake found a species of spider living on the ice. I have never felt any affection for spiders, they have just too many legs for me. On the other hand, I have often admired their webs, especially in the early mornings when against the rising sun dewdrops, caught on the thread, glistened like crystals.

Ake showed me some of the spiders under a microscope and then I realised how exquisitely they were made and how velvety their body was. I painted a few under a magnifying glass but I found it a great strain on my eyes. The only mammals we saw were hyrax and small rodents, though we observed the spoor of a leopard at an altitude of 14,000 feet. Most of the time between 9 March and 18 April we had splendid weather high above a sea of clouds on which the peaks and moorlands seemed to float. While the sun shone it was pleasantly hot but when night fell it became so cold that even Aquavit and hot-water bottles could not keep us warm in our small tents. I love wine but not hard drinks: in the N.F.D. from necessity I learned to drink beer, for in a hot climate one loses so much fluid by perspiration that to replace it with the necessary quantity of wine, let alone spirits, would have disastrous side effects. But here, during the bitter nights of the Ruwenzori, Aquavit was a real tonic – and also the Swedish tradition of giving endless toasts before one was allowed to drink the warming draughts, helped to cement our friendships.

We all found so much fascinating work that we were sad when the time came to leave but, on the day we finished packing up, the weather broke and a heavy snowstorm reduced visibility almost to nil.

We took one guide and set off, hoping that our tracks would help the other guide who was following with the porters. We proceeded slowly, keeping in touch with the second group by shouting. The ground was difficult to walk over even under normal conditions, but with the present blizzard it was terrible. Several times we had to slide over the slippery moss-covered rocks, often sixty feet deep. This tobogganing was alright for us but we were very worried as to how our porters, with their heavy loads, would be able to manage, particularly as we could no longer keep in touch with them by shouting. Our guide suggested that we should continue to a rocky cliff where we could spend the night, and where we thought that the other guide would catch up with us. After several hours of slithering and stumbling, we reached our refuge. I had hoped for a comfortable cave so was disappointed when I realised that we should have to spend the night on this very narrow ledge, six feet wide and forty-five feet long and cut into a precipitous cliff which fell into a raging river 100 yards below.

We lit a fire of soggy grass and crouched around it in our soaking clothes, listening anxiously for shouts from the porters. It was after midnight when at last we heard faint calls. We flashed our torches and were greatly relieved when, one by one, the porters staggered on to the ledge and flung down their heavy loads. They had had a very hard trek but next day we parted the best of friends, for these good-natured men were absolutely delighted when we told them they could keep their blankets and their boots as souvenirs of the trip.

The Swedish team now split up, its members going off in different directions; only Ake, Olaf and I returned to Kenya to pursue our studies on Mount Elgon. When we reached the home of friends who lived there, and who had been harbouring Pippin, I was very pleased to find him happy and fit. He and I had been through a lot together and there seemed to be a special bond between us. When he saw me making preparations for our departure he never left me for a second, and this time he had the satisfaction of coming with us.

By now I had recorded about 700 plants, and of these I had found the alpine plants and the flowering trees the most interesting to paint. Once I had added the flora of Mount Elgon to my collection I made up my mind that I would concentrate on painting Africans in their traditional costumes, while I could still hope to find people wearing authentic ornaments. We had to wait to collect our porters so Ake, Olaf and I drove 100 miles north to Kacheliba, an area which is little visited.

One morning two men of the Kadam tribe walked into our camp. They carried spears and were naked except for elaborate head-dresses. They were Nilo-Hamites, tall and slender, and obviously not used to foreign visitors. One had a particularly striking head-dress: a mud-cake chignon mixed from his hair, grease and bluish clay was moulded into a hood which covered his shoulders and ended up at a point half-way down his spine. A few ostrich feathers were stuck into small holders made of dried cow-tits which had been inserted into the mud before it hardened. These indicated the man's rank, age group and status of warrior. His companion's head-dress looked like a crown of feathers neatly woven into a thick ring. Its design was one I have never seen since.

We could only communicate with our eyes and by gestures but the men were quick on the uptake and both agreed to allow me to make portraits of them and to photograph them. In return they received tobacco and money.

Later we set off for Mount Elgon which stands on the border between Uganda and Kenya. It is an extinct volcano that rises to 14,000 feet and is known for its unique alpine flora. The ascent through bamboo forests right up to the crater's rim was easy, from there we looked into the crater floor which was a few miles wide. At its centre was a tiny island which lay between a hot spring and the source of the Turkwell River. This seemed an ideal camping place, so we made our way down to it. If we wanted to warm our feet on cold evenings we could put them into the bubbling water, or if we wanted a refreshing drink – get it straight from the cold stream. Pippin enjoyed the warm stream but at sunset he came into my tent to be safe from the buffaloes and other animals that arrived during the night to drink. During the three weeks we stayed on Mount Elgon I found and painted many plants that were new to me and learned a lot from Olaf about botany.

When I parted from my Swedish friends I still had some time in hand before George's return from the Ethiopian border. Thanks to the District Commissioner at Kitale I was invited to Kapenguria, the administrative centre of the East Suk. There the agricultural officer and the D.C. kindly found models for me. Since I could not speak Suk I thought I would be able to keep my sitters interested if I sat them facing me and looked them straight in the eye but, in fact, having hardly ever seen a foreigner before, they were as much intrigued by my blonde hair and blue eyes as I was by their appearance.

I found the women very shy but nevertheless easier to deal with than the men, who were inquisitive and apt to misinterpret my admiration for their coiffure.

Later I painted some of the Elgeyo people who lived near to Kapenguria. My studio was close to the District Officer's office, which enabled me to choose my sitters from among the many people who daily crowded in to see him. My first model, a local chief, wore a magnificent coat of blue monkey fur. By now I had become so enthusiastic about my painting plan that I wanted to record the fifty main tribes, and, if possible, some of the fifty-two sub-tribes. To do this I needed George's consent to dividing my time between him and my painting safaris: he agreed.

That settled, the next step was to buy a car for I could not travel by bus with all my paraphernalia. With the little money I had, I bought a second-hand station wagon large enough to carry my painting equipment and my camping kit. I was very proud of my first car but I only went a short distance in it before it was surrounded by a cloud of smoke and I expected it to explode at any moment. I feared I would never drive it again but, in the event, it was repaired and survived for a time. Being mobile enabled me to visit several administrative posts. The more I painted Africans and their traditional ornaments, the more aware I became that it was important to record their fast-disappearing culture.

During the part of my life which now opened out before me I learned a great deal about the complexitites of tribal customs and witnessed the transition from the old ways of life to new ones influenced by the West. The most important, as well as the most secret, time in the life of these Africans was that of the circumcision ritual. The candidates were circumcised in groups, or individually, according to the custom of the tribe. The operation on the genitals was only a small part of the ritual, though the self-control and courage shown by the initiate was tested by it. It was, however, the seclusion that followed the act which was regarded as of the utmost importance in forming the character of the individual. During this period, which might go on for weeks or even up to two years, no one is allowed to see the candidate except the tutor who is preparing him for his future duties to the tribe. In the event I was lucky, for I met two circumcision candidates of the Njemps tribe who were undergoing seclusion. They evidently had never seen a white woman and their curiosity was such that they agreed to pose for their portrait. Later these paintings were my stock in trade to help me with less cooperative chiefs by convincing them that all I wanted was to record their traditional customs for future generations, who might otherwise never know about them. But if I hoped to include all the tribes of Kenya in my record, I needed also support from the Government.

Luck was again on my side when I met the Commissioner for Social Welfare and showed him my pictures and told him of my plans. He was so interested that he took the sketches to Nairobi to show them to members of the Government. In consequence on 14 February 1949 I signed a contract to paint twenty tribes which were known to be losing interest in their traditional rituals and in the ornaments that were symbols of them.

I was to hand in my portraits within eighteen months. Meanwhile, I was allocated £1,000 to cover all my expenses except for petrol. I was instructed to notify the administrator of the area I intended to visit three weeks in advance. The authorities would then summon Africans who owned authentic costumes and ask them to be ready for my arrival. In each location I was provided with an interpreter and a police escort. When I had selected my models, the chief and I would decide on the pay and the date at which the sitter would come to my camp. Many of them lived far away and so we had to work out a schedule, but the concept of time does not come easily to Africans and, as a result, I had invariably to wait a day or two for my sitter to turn up, and then upset the queue. I had allowed two days to paint each model; to keep to the programme, I was often obliged to paint the features quickly and outline the many ornaments, dabbing colour samples on to the sketch. Then, after dark, by the flicker of a kerosene lamp I completed all the details of the ornaments.

I soon found that the older people knew the symbolism of the ornaments, which provided information about the status of the wearers and details of their personal history. For those who could interpret them, they signified whether a young person had been circumcised or not, or whether he was then undergoing the initiation period; they also indicated the phase before marriage. Apart from declaring the wearer's age group, they gave evidence of his profession. Warrior, witchdoctor, sorcerer, circumciser, rain-maker, prophet, blacksmith, potter, judge, elder – all had their individual ornaments and so did widows and barren women.

I asked each person separately about the significance of the ornaments. If several agreed on the answer I assumed I was on safe ground, but if they contradicted each other I did not paint them, however picturesque they might be. I was saddened by discovering that none of the young people showed any interest in their traditional culture. Instead they regarded the wearing of such ornaments as a stigma. Missionaries must take much of the blame for this attitude; they were the first to bring education to the Africans, but in doing so wiped out what they regarded as the customs of savages, not perceiving that cultures evolve from the religion and racial history of the people involved and from the climatic conditions in which they live.

During these rather lonely weeks I found Pippin a wonderful companion. When I lived in Austria, though I always had dogs, I had had to share them with the family. With Pippin it was different as he was very much my personal friend. He was also of the greatest help in entertaining my models, who had never before seen a Cairn terrier, and watched him alertly.

After I had been painting for some months I realised that the tribes the Government had listed as those which were changing their way of life, and thus most likely to give up their traditional ornaments, were by no means the only ones who were copying the Western way of life.

In view of this it was agreed that the District Officer and I would choose the tribes to be added to the record. This would obviously mean expanding my list, taking longer over my task, and therefore I would require more money. As I believed that money would sooner or later be available for such an important task, and that it was the last opportunity to record, at least in paintings, these unique tribal cultures, I determined to continue even if I had to economise on essentials.

Eating I came to regard as merely a necessity to enable me to carry on. For weeks I lived on eggs, vegetables and bananas, the cheapest food I could buy locally. Often I was so absorbed by my work that it was only the onset of a headache which reminded me I had eaten nothing since dawn. I worried much more about Pippin's diet, since meat and bones were not easy to get. Luckily he was very popular among the Africans, who told me where the livestock were slaughtered and after that he never lacked a good meal. Even so, he seemed to be off colour and started to have repeated nose bleeds. I took him to the nearest vet at Nyeri, who gave him injections which stopped the bleeding for a while but when it recurred and the injections were repeated, they had little effect and I realised that Pippin was getting weaker and weaker.

I now camped in the Embu district at the foot of Mount Kenya to paint the Mbere tribe. They were famous for their dancing. For days and nights they would continue their violent acrobatic movements to the frantic rhythm of enormous drums. The chief had offered me a rest house made of reeds and grass, which was the sole cool place in this treeless plain. The region was within George's game control area and one day he turned up unexpectedly for the weekend. By then Pippin was too weak to come with us on our afternoon stroll and that night he died.

It seemed providential that George should have come just then to help me get over this sad event. We spent the rest of the night taking Pippin to a small patch of forest where we dug his grave under a tree. With him I buried part of myself, he had been my companion and friend through very difficult years.

Next morning George had to leave, I felt so wretched during the following days that I could not paint; but soon a game scout arrived. He brought me a baby serval cat, which had been found abandoned on a road and which George had sent me. It was the size of a small kitten, a real charmer and I fell for it at once, but it was no replacement for Pippin.

When my stay at Mbere ended George came to help me pack up and move to where the Chuka, the next tribe on my list, lived. On the way, a friend invited us to spend a night in his guest house – a rondavel built of mud-bricks, with a grass-thatched roof.

When I introduced the serval cat to the family I observed that our hostess did not take to it, indeed I felt that we obviously should not have brought it with us. Everyone tried their best to mitigate our embarrassment, but all the same we had an uncomfortable dinner and retired early. Now it started to rain so heavily that soon the new guest house was a foot under water and the kitten's sleeping box awash. I rescued her and took her into my bed but the continual drumming of the rain on the roof frightened her so much that she made a mess all over the sheets and blankets. Anyone who knows how smelly a domestic cat's excrement can be, let alone that of a wild cat, can imagine our concern. There was no rag around to use for cleaning up so I had to do the best I could with old newspapers and magazines. Finally, I carried the large messy pile through the storm to the outside toilet. I had to make so many trips that I was soaked to the skin and the hole was filled right up to the brim. The rain continued remorselessly until seven inches had fallen, then it stopped and it was fine when we made our way over to breakfast at the big house. At that moment I saw our hostess coming very rapidly out of the toilet. I could judge what she felt by her expression. My embarrassment was such that despite our apologies and promises to replace the sheets and blankets we felt we should leave at once, so as to order new bedding as soon as we could.

At the Chuka location a group of people had assembled, all hoping to be chosen as models. I selected a few but was feeling so ill that I took my temperature. It was 103°F and, as my symptoms suggested that I was in for a bout of malaria, George insisted that I should go on with him to Isiolo. I arranged with the chief that my painting session should take place later.

While I was recovering, George was asked to find a route with enough water and grazing to enable 1,800 Turkana to make their way along it with their livestock in order to reach the Lake Rudolf area.

During the war these Turkana had settled, illegally, around Isiolo – thus infringing the water rights of the local Somali; now they were to be returned to their own country. The Government was already preparing to evacuate the old people and children by lorry via Kitale to Lodwar. Simultaneously, they were arranging to provide food dumps at intervals along the track which George recommended as most suitable for the great trek of the able-bodied with their cattle. The move was not popular amongst the tribesmen, the elders prophesied that it would never take place, and because of this most of the Turkana were reluctant to co-operate in any of the plans made for them.

To cope with possible administrative problems at the other end, a young assistant was seconded to George. I wanted to join this recce as I hoped to find interesting models to paint in the remote areas through which we should pass. After sending our pack animals ahead to Wamba, the last place to which we could travel by car, we loaded our Chevrolet pick-up with provisions, medicines, tents, bedding rolls, camp tables and chairs, a canvas bath, kitchen utensils, rifles and ammunition, clothes, lamps, a faltboat, forty-gallon drums to be used as water containers, phials and glass plates for collecting blood smears, glycerine and iodine for preserving specimens, presses for collecting plants, my painting kit and some books. We covered this load with a ground-sheet after which our domestic staff and the game scouts climbed on top. Overloaded as we were, we were surprised when we collected the assistant that he should insist on taking a 'wooden throne' along. This soon became a joke, for at intervals he would stop us to look for a shady place 'with a nice view' where he could establish his throne.

When we reached Wamba the young man looked contemptuously at our mules and commented that he was used to riding thoroughbreds.

George had recently acquired a white mule known as 'Shaitani', a word which means 'devil' in Swahili. He suggested that the assistant should ride this beast. He agreed and mounted it proudly but before he was even seated the mule dashed into the nearby river and threw his rider, then walked innocently up the bank. The assistant mounted Shaitani again and the mule ambled quietly along until he reached a thorn bush where he bucked, depositing his rider into the thorns.

Wiping his bleeding head and cursing all mules the assistant announced that in spite of everything he was in fact a first-class horseman. Hearing this George decided to 'allow' him to ride Shaitani for the rest of the safari. The poor young man was very unhappy but his pride would not allow him to protest. He still tried to show off although he often landed on the ground with the mule looking down at him quizzically. Like all other animals a mule can sense the attitude of a human being towards him. Eventually Shaitani was so displeased with his rider that one night he bolted. It took him four days to reach Isiolo where he arrived very fit in spite of having had to trot for most of the way through lion country.

We didn't know it but the assistant had his private troubles at the time which no doubt accounted for his talent for provoking rows. In the end George decided to send him home. For my part, I felt some sympathy with him because I too had felt superior when I first tried to ride a mule, after having been taught classic horsemanship in Vienna. I watched George sitting like a sack of potatoes and bouncing up and down with every step the mule took but he never fell off whereas I, determined to stick to my much grander way of riding, was constantly thrown.

We were riding ahead of the donkeys to keep the track clear of wild animals; our pace was slow, it was the hottest time of day and I became very drowsy. Suddenly I felt a bump and a rhino and her calf brushed against my mule and rushed off at top speed. I fell heavily, my spine landing on a sharp rock. George, who was in front, returned rapidly and helped me to remount my frightened mule. I ached all over and seemed to be partially paralysed but he impressed on me the need to reach the next water-hole before dark, telling me that the last time he had camped in the spot where we were he had been hunting a man-eater who had killed a Somali. He had not seen the beast but, next morning, had found a lion's pugmarks between his camp bed and the tent ropes. This story convinced me that however painful it might be, I must go on, for anything was better than to settle where a marauding man-eater lurked.

At last we arrived at the water-hole and though I had a restless night and ached all over, next morning we went on through terribly dry country, where, however often we made experimental digs in dry river-beds, we never found any water. What we did find were fossilised trees, whose trunks were up to two feet in diameter, showing that at one time this area had been thickly forested. Eventually we reached the Sugota Valley, a former lake bed and one of the hottest places in Africa. It is flanked on either side by steep walls of rock, which prevent any cool wind from reaching it. Here I again searched for fossils but did not find any, which surprised me since in prehistoric times the Sugota Valley was connected with both Lake Rudolf and the Nile, and Lake Rudolf was rich in fossils.

We continued our way towards Lodwar over the lava desert. Suddenly I became dizzy and was just about to fall off my mule when George caught me. He took my temperature, which was 104°F, so he wrapped me in wet blankets while our African staff pitched camp on the shadeless plain. We spent a night there and next morning, to my surprise, I was well again.

Our next lap took us over a plateau strewn with lava, where there was no grass for the donkeys. Luckily the moon was nearly full so we were able to travel by night, which was essential as during the day donkeys were vulnerable to heat-stroke.

At Kangetet we met the District Officer from Lodwar. Everyone agreed that it would be quite impossible to move a large number of people, together with their livestock, along the route we had taken. Leaving the men to discuss alternative plans, I decided to paint some Turkana women, whose costumes and hair-do's differed from the Turkana I had already painted.

Twelve days after my recent attack of fever I again ran a high temperature. We then decided that I must be suffering from relapsing fever, a tick-borne disease and, thinking it over, I even recalled that I had been bitten by a tick, which had resulted in an icy chill lasting for several hours, while camping in the grass shelter of the Mbere Plain. If our diagnosis were correct we could now plan on my running a high temperature and feeling ill at regular intervals and could arrange that on every twelfth day we should reach a shady camp site.

We were in true Turkana country and I could well understand why those who had reached the Isiolo area preferred to remain there. We returned by a different route but it too was devoid of sufficient grazing or water-holes to make it possible for a large number of people and their livestock to follow it.

George suggested to the authorities that the only practical alternative was to move very small groups with their essential livestock during the rains. The remaining livestock would have to be sold at Isiolo and compensated for at Lodwar. This solution was not adopted so the prophecy of the Turkana elders, that the move would not take place, came true.

I now consulted a doctor in Nairobi about my intermittent attacks of fever, he confirmed our diagnosis of relapsing fever and treated me with injections of arsenic.

Soon after I was well again George and I received an invitation to the farewell party of the outgoing Governor at Wajir. This *beau geste* fort, sometimes then described as 'One Outpost of the British Empire', stands in a sandy plain. It is the main defence post in hundreds of miles, and also the sole source of fresh water in a desert area.

Wajir has some twenty wells, they are circular holes about sixty feet deep, chiselled through the solid limestone. Their diameter is so small that it is hard to imagine how they could have been drilled without mechanical help. One guess is that a child was lowered in a basket to do the excavation.

Besides these wells, there are large catchment dams some distance away. They are extremely solid constructions, far beyond the ability of the present Somali population. A legend describes early inhabitants of the area as belonging to a giant race named the Wandirr – perhaps they were responsible for these feats of engineering?

In the large square courtyard of the fort a marquee had been erected. All the administrative staff of the N.F.D. were present, but Alys Reece and I were the only representatives of the wives. Many Somalis were massed at the end of the courtyard and after

an address to the Governor a small number of Somalis ran forward, shouting their war cry and raising their spears. As they
approached him, they came faster and faster, till finally they threw
their spears, with great accuracy, at his feet. This group was
followed by others, until all present had performed the rite.
Meanwhile, the Governor stood without twitching an eyelid as
these fearsome weapons fell within inches of his toes. During the
festivities I painted some of the Somalis, among whom I found
some very interesting models.

On our return to Isiolo I resumed my interrupted painting
session of the Chuka. This tribe lives at the base of Mount
Kenya. From where my camp was sited only the forest belt
separated us from the moorlands and glaciers; so, one weekend,
when George came to visit me, we decided to spend a day walking
up the mountain. We followed an old track made by members of
the Chogoria Mission, the oldest mission in the area and renowned
for its excellent, and very popular, hospital.

We entered the forest which was magnificent, then after a few
hours we came to bamboo and later to open scrub. The higher
we got, the greater was the variety of flowers and birds, while the
special aroma, typical of high altitudes, was intoxicating.

In the stillness and immensity of the view, we walked on and
on. Finally George said it was time to turn back, but I had seen
an emerald tarn which I simply *had* to reach, and as well some
ruby-coloured everlastings cushioned on silvery leaves which I
had to pick, so I paid no attention. Seeing this, he sensibly took
the one course likely to bring me back to reality, he started for
home. I went on for a while and then suddenly realising I was
alone, my mood changed from elation to fear. I looked at the
setting sun, decided that this was no time for meditation and
hurried off and caught up with George. After such a perfect day
we were surprised to hear the rumblings of an approaching
thunderstorm. By the time it broke we were already in the forest,
where darkness fell quickly and it was not long before we were
benighted. Hurrying downhill, we soon lost the tracks we had
made on our way up and as we could see no landmarks there was
nothing to do but wait till it got light.

Sitting on the grass was equivalent to sitting on a running

flood, so we squatted close together for warmth and resigned ourselves to a wet, cold and hungry night.

Suddenly George remembered that in the past on one such occasion he had cut the rubber soles of his sandals into strips, lit them and burned them like torches, both for warmth and to keep wild animals away. He now suggested that I should sacrifice my sandals and although I knew it would mean walking barefoot over rough ground in the morning, I agreed since I recognised that I was responsible for our ordeal.

The hours passed, the rain poured and from the noises we heard, the animals around us seemed to be more attracted than repelled by our torches. It was not until the first shimmer of dawn broke that the rain ceased and we were able to set off again, very stiff after our night-long squat.

However varied and interesting our life often was, it was also very restless and insecure and I had another miscarriage, the third now by three husbands. I badly wanted a child, but evidently had not the mentality of a brooding hen, and I felt very distressed. As if to help me over my dilemma we were given a newly born rock hyrax, an animal that looks like a marmot though zoologists insist that by its feet and its teeth it must be related to rhinos and elephants. I called it Pati after the famous opera singer because, at first, I believed that she was a tree hyrax, a nocturnal animal with a very loud cry; however, she proved to be a rock hyrax, diurnal and not noisy but the name stuck to her. She was so young when she came to us that she adapted easily to our life. She never gave us any trouble for she was naturally very clean and there was no need to house-train her, in fact she took at once to the seat of the WC, no doubt it replaced the cliff she would normally have used in the wild. So addicted did she become to this toilet that when we went on safari we were obliged to take an improvised WC with us, otherwise she refused to do her duty.

Like all hyrax Pati was a vegetarian who loved bananas, paw-paw and mangoes which she often stole from my plate. Drink, however, was her real weakness and whenever she found a bottle she toppled it over and pulled out the cork.

Pati accompanied us on all our safaris, sitting on my shoulder when I rode; she also, when necessary, went to sea in a dhow but her favourite trips were to Mount Kenya.

It was in 1951 that George got a report of poaching on the Chandlers Falls up the Uaso Nyiro river. These falls are rarely visited and can only be reached along a very rough track, close to the river which, at this time, was running very low.

We set out at once and as we passed a limestone deposit I dug out some fossilised spindle shells which I sent to the Nairobi Museum.

The country here was flat with small groups of acacia trees giving shade to the local wild life, which included elephants, zebras, reticulated giraffes and buffaloes.

The falls were spectacular even in the dry season, with a rush of water falling eighty feet.

We clambered down a narrow path and entered a natural vault about ten feet wide, half a mile long and high enough to be able to walk upright comfortably. This might have been caused by a fault in the rocky wall flanking the river which was almost level with the floor of the vault. In the water we saw several crocs, also a number of snares left by poachers.

We had not gone very far when there was a deafening roar from the direction of the falls and immediately the water rose covering the floor of the vault. Fearing to be trapped, we splashed back as fast as we could.

When we reached the falls they had changed alarmingly, dark red waves carrying trees and logs were thundering down the eighty feet with such force that the foam rose to a high level. The situation was getting worse by the minute and we realised that if we were to avoid drowning we had not a second to lose. We heaved one another up to the cliff above the vault, groping for the smallest ledge and clinging to any projection which we could grasp. It is amazing what acrobatic feats one can achieve when faced by death. The cause of the flood must have been the breaking of the overdue rains up-country.

On our way home we learned of excessive poaching of elephant tusks at the Lorian swamp, where the drought had been so severe that wild animals as well as domestic stock were dying of thirst and poachers exploited these tragedies. George was now asked to recover the tusks of the dead elephants – a gruesome task.

The Lorian swamp, about eight miles long and fed by the Uaso Nyiro, is known as a paradise for elephants; it lies 150 miles from Isiolo – half way to Wajir, in desert country. When the Uaso Nyiro dries up, the thirty-five wells of the Lorian are the only water supply for about a thousand square miles around. During the last few weeks the drought had forced thousands of Somalis to walk long distances with their livestock to reach those wells, and many of them had become too weak and had died along the way. Already, many miles before we reached the Lorian, the ground was littered with decaying camels, cattle, sheep and goats, and as we approached the wells the stench became nauseating. The carcasses lay between the dried-up reeds on the cracked mud and however carefully we drove, it was impossible to avoid a few of them.

After the Somalis had walked enormous distances with their stock, they were then forced to wait, often for several days without shade, until the people who had arrived before them gave way at the wells; to make matters worse there were also elephants competing for the water.

In particular, there was one bull, desperate with thirst, who waited persistently every evening at the last of the thirty-five wells which still held water. It was thirty feet deep; the Somalis stood on a ladder, ten men above each other, bucketing up the water which was poured into troughs for their stock. As soon as they emerged with their water, the elephant took it and chased the men, grabbing at their wet loincloths. There had been three near-accidents when the elephant had trampled earth into the well and buried the men below, in order to hurry up the Somalis. Abdi Ogli, a famous Somali chief of outstanding character, had only just prevented a mutiny. Though he sympathised with the animals, he begged George to shoot this bull.

While waiting after dark for the elephant to arrive, we strolled along the dried-up river-bed and found three elephants next to a camel. They had been trapped in the hardening mud which they had been sucking while it was still liquid. All were dead with only their heads above the mud, except for the camel. The locals told us that it had been sinking deeper and deeper during the last thirty-six days. Unable to defend itself against vultures, it now opened its eyes and seemed to ask for the *coup de grâce*. George shot it instantly.

We then watched a dried-up muddy pool full of wriggling or decaying catfish, on which heron were busy at their unpleasant task.

Instead of the gay chatter which usually echoes around wells, there was now a sinister silence. The sun was fierce and everybody was half dead from thirst.

Soon after dark the elephant appeared, sniffing for water; he stampeded through the exhausted Somalis, making straight for the well. As soon as he stopped I held up the torch and George killed him with a brain shot. Crashing to the ground, he buried a live sheep which had been too weak to move away.

Now the tense stillness changed into laughter and singing and dancing, and George was thanked with heartfelt gratitude.

During the following days we helped transport newcomers to the well to save them the last few miles' walk. We also collected twelve pairs of tusks from dead elephants.

One morning we were woken up by jubilant shouting, 'The river is coming!' Like everyone else we rushed to the Uaso Nyiro expecting to hear a headwave roaring along. Instead, we saw a thin trickle meandering slowly through the sand, filling holes and cracks. The Somalis, drunk with joy, were lining the banks of the river with their stock.

We left, hoping that the people and their animals were safe. How wrong we were! The rains broke with such force that soon George received a message asking his help in bringing food to them, for now they were marooned by a ten-mile-wide lake – and again starving. Lorries had been sent with food but they had got stuck in mud. Aircraft had dropped food but most of it had splashed into the water. Donkeys and camels, loaded with food, were drenched and their loads soaked. George, who had a tiny dinghy, was the last hope.

Most of the 150-mile track was muddy and we were just – but only just – able to reach the lake. But here, as there was nobody at the other side to meet us, we were finally defeated. It was the very same spot where only three weeks earlier we had watched the Somalis collapsing from thirst. Africa has a reputation for being a continent of extremes, our experience of the Lorian swamp confirmed this.

During the next few months I painted the tribes in the west of Kenya but, owing to the heavy rain, the light in my tent was very poor and I strained my eyes and was obliged to stop painting for a while.

When my eyes had recovered I went to Fort Victoria on the Kenya-Uganda border to paint the Samia tribe. They live close to a big swamp which only recently had been cleared of the tsetse fly. The only Europeans in the area were three missionaries. I stayed for one night at their mission which looked more like a sinister fort than a haven of peace, and lying on my hard and prickly straw-filled sack I realised what an austere life these ascetic priests lived.

A month later I accompanied George to Mandera on the Ethiopian border. On my first morning there I woke to the muffled sound of wooden bells and saw a line of camels, tethered nose to tail, silhouetted against the horizon. On their backs they carried their owners' possessions, loaded between two crossed sticks. Seeing them advancing through this desert country one understood why they had long been named 'the ships of the desert'.

The country here had the austere and natural harshness of an endless plain, on which only a meagre scrub grew through the sand. The Daua River was the boundary between Kenya and Ethiopia and also the lifeline of the local people and their stock, for it was the one place where they could quench their thirst.

Thousands of camels belonging to the Dagodia-Masere Somali tribe were driven here to drink. In spite of the presence of many crocodiles, they stood knee-deep in the water gurgling in competition with the bleating of the goats.

Along the frontier were a few outposts; El Roba, a picturesque look-out sited on great rocks, and the impressive forts of El Wak and Mulka Mari behind whose thick walls all the military equipment needed to defend the region was stored.

In the Daua we were surprised to find the same rare turtle (*Trionyx genus*) which we had seen at Lake Rudolf and which it had been believed existed only there and in the Nile. Its length from head to tail is about three feet, it has a long thin neck, and a third of its shell, the part near its tail, is not solid like the rest but rubbery.

While in this area we visited some tombs at Harange and that of the holy Sheikh Habaemur. They were almost hidden by strips of leather which pilgrims had tied to surrounding bushes.

From the northern end of Kenya I travelled to the south to paint the Taveta tribe on the border of Tanzania. While there I called on Colonel Grogan, now seventy, who was famous for his great walk, fifty years earlier, from the Cape to Cairo. We discussed the question of the colour bar; in his opinion what was more significant was the culture bar, which in fact existed all over the world.

All my life I have been struck by the clash of cultures and also, of course, by the transition from the traditional culture to a modern culture. For instance, an Arab I painted had sent his daughters to be educated in London while his father kept his wives in purdah. And in a different context, there was the occasion when George had to shoot two lions who had been raiding cattle. He and I and an English couple went out in a lorry to wait for them. As dusk fell George and I were tense, watching every moving shadow, listening to the slightest crackle of a twig, while one of our guests knitted and the other played chess with himself.

Tastes differ; only one thing is certain, people get out of life exactly what they put into it.

9

Across the Sahara
and a Sad Return
to Kenya

Government regulations demanded that officers should have a break at intervals and moreover that some of their leave should be spent abroad; this was enforced particularly if they were working in the Tropics. George had paid no attention to these rules, and had accumulated leave amounting to two years as he had not left Kenya for twenty-seven years. In 1953 he was virtually ordered to go overseas.

To make the change less of a shock I suggested that, rather than fly to England, we should motor through the Sahara. We started in March, although this was dangerously near to the sandstorm season when the area is closed for six months. To be on the safe side we availed ourselves of the arrangement by which travellers pay a deposit at the French Embassy in Nairobi which entitles them to get petrol at various forts (one can obviously not carry enough fuel for a 3,000-mile journey), and also ensures that a rescue operation would be mounted should one be stranded – the deposit for this service is refunded if one gets through safely. We chose the route through the centre of the Sahara, which appealed to us more than the east or west routes.

We had a trailer to carry our camping kit and George took firearms, hoping to hunt Derby eland in Chad, and moufflon and other game on the way.

Crossing into Uganda we had trouble over the rifles. If we paid for the bond which would have allowed us to take them along we would be left with no money. After an interminable argument, which did not seem to be getting us anywhere, I burst into tears. Displeased, George gave me a surreptitious kick but the heart of the customs officer softened and after sealing the rifles and making us promise not to use them, he allowed us to take them with us. At frontier posts further along our route when any difficulties arose, George kicked me again but this time he whispered, 'Start crying at once'. My tears worked wonders.

We drove several hundred miles through the Ituri Forest, whose dense green walls nearly gave me claustrophobia. For one night we were the guests of Dr and Mrs Pitman, an American couple who lived in a remote rest-house, and had a fabulous collection of early wood carvings from the west coast. They were there to study Pygmies.

They took us to a Pygmy village where we watched the little people hammering bark into cloth material on which they used herbal dyes and afterwards painted interesting designs. We also saw a Pygmy hunt. The men waited with their poisoned arrows by a net which had been stretched across part of the forest and into which the women, acting as beaters, drove the game. From a very early age Pygmy boys are trained to be good marksmen; they form a circle, in the middle of which stands a youngster who flings a ball attached to a string past them, and at this they aim. The Pygmies are a very brave race, the men being prepared to walk right under an elephant to pierce it to the heart with their tiny spears. One evening we heard the Pygmy labour gang singing a chorus, in which each person was allotted one note which he sang at the required moment to make a tune. I wondered whether more sophisticated people could achieve such perfect synchronisation without a conductor.

Emerging from the Ituri Forest we entered bush land; here we saw a number of knee-high pagodas, some with as many as seven tiers. They were termite mounds, apparently designed to offer the maximum surface capable of catching moisture – hard as stone, when crushed, they were used to surface roads.

At Fort Crampel we were offered a young, banded mongoose

and had no option but to take him since Crampel, as we named him, adopted us on sight, jumping from his owner's hand into mine and making it plain that from now on we were his foster parents. We never regretted little Crampel's decision and became very fond of him.

We went on to Fort Archambault which stands equidistant from the Atlantic and the Indian Oceans. It is a most expensive place because everything, from a reel of cotton to a chair, has to be flown in at great cost. We had hoped that here George would have a chance of shooting a Derby eland, so we asked the Game Department to recommend a white hunter. Next morning a man carrying a teapot called on us. The teapot appeared to be his only safari equipment. He proceeded to tell us the most fantastic hunting yarns, which would not have convinced a greenhorn. When he discovered that George was a member of the Kenya Game Department I felt quite sorry for him.

We travelled on through French Equatoria, where the introductions given me by Louis Leakey asking tribal dignitaries to allow me to take photographs, proved most useful. We saw bottle-shaped mud huts, whose walls had been beautifully decorated and we met members of the Kim tribe, who wore picturesque hairstyles and splendid ornaments and lived between Koumra and Lai. I was even able to take photographs of some Banda girls in their circumcision costumes near Kembe.

When we reached the French Cameroons we saw the mud huts belonging to the Guizas, perched on the top of high hills and well hidden by boulders. These people, and also the Mofous who live between Meri and Mora, are excellent weavers. As in Kenya, the weaving is only done north of the Equator and carried out by men, using primitive looms; they make strips about two inches wide which are later sewn together to provide loose-fitting garments that hang to the knees. A craft at which the Podoco tribe near Mora are adept is making great pots that are shoulder-high and resemble those made by the Hausa in French Niger. It was only possible for me to photograph the women of the Fulani, Hausa and Madara tribes and those of the Bolewa and Kanuri in Niger thanks to the cooperation of the local Emirs. All these women have very elaborate hairstyles which I was anxious to record. I was particularly interested because of the difficulty of finding people still wearing traditional clothing.

Emir Muhamadu of Fika was extremely kind, he even posed for me himself simply to reassure the more primitive people who were still suspicious of the camera.

Sadly Crampel suddenly became very ill. We went to Kano in Nigeria to consult a vet but he was not able to save the little mongoose, who had perhaps eaten a poisonous beetle. I was most upset to lose him as he gave us so much pleasure.

Kano is famous for its indigo dyes and for its ancient city walls. In its market are deep circular wells, in which the dyed cotton is rinsed. It is also rumoured that unwanted persons have been known to be thrown into them.

While there I bought myself some desert cloth, as worn by the locals. It consisted of a double body-length of cotton with a hole in the middle to put one's head through, so that the material fell loosely from the shoulders to the feet. At the time I thought I looked very peculiar in it but today it would be accepted as a fashionable kaftan.

The next stage of our journey was through flat country; the only apparently moving objects on this monotonous plain were bushes blown by the wind into bizarre movements that made them look as if they were performing a devils' dance.

In Algeria, near Guezzamir and in Guezzam, we saw many prehistoric rock engravings of antelopes and giraffes, which proved that in those days the present desert must have been covered with vegetation.

As we were lunching in the middle of a vast sandy plain, devoid of any landmark, a sand grouse suddenly appeared and made straight for the coolest place – the shade under the car. Here, exhausted, she collapsed. I took her on to my lap, sprinkled water over her and into her beak but she remained apparently lifeless. When we set off again I kept her on my knees, holding her wings splayed out for coolness. After a while she opened her eyes, shivered and took off, flying back into nowhere.

During another of our luncheon picnics a noble-looking Tuareg appeared from behind a rock, riding on a beautiful white camel – obviously a thoroughbred. The rider's face was veiled by typical indigo-coloured cloth but his bearing was impressive. We greeted each other in silence, then he dismounted and offered us camel milk in an embossed copper bowl. We had nothing to give him in return except food out of a tin, which made us look rather shabby. We could not communicate by speech, yet we felt that there was a real contact. After a while, like the sand grouse, the Tuareg left us for the unknown.

Later we passed a few flimsy tents which belonged to nomadic Tuaregs. We were invited to enter some of them and I was amazed to see amongst the nomads' few possessions wooden chests studded with silver. Except for the children, all the Tuaregs were veiled. The indigo of their robes contrasted vividly with the red, yellow and green hills leading up to the Hogar Mountains which were dark-red and eroded into shapes that suggested columns raking the sky.

We followed a rough track to the plateau of Asekrem, which stands at 8,400 feet. Here we came upon a small hermitage. It had been the home of the celebrated Père de Foucauld who, in his youth, had shocked his superior officers by his wild night-life and had been sent to the Sahara on a punitive expedition against the Tuaregs to cool off. The grandeur of the desert overwhelmed him and eventually, after a spell in a monastery, he settled in the Hogar Mountains where he lived as a hermit. He loved the Tuaregs and was greatly respected by them. Tragically, during the First World War, he was murdered here. By a strange coincidence, when we reached Paris, we saw an exhibition of his writings, from which it was plain that the affection between the Tuaregs and Charles de Foucauld arose from their mutual belief in God and their sharing the simple life of the desert.

Next we visited the place where the bleaching bones of the gallant Tuaregs, mowed down in 1902 as they charged on their camels into French rifle fire, lay in a great heap in the sun. This sight made us understand why the French did not seem to be very popular in this area.

Up to now we had not had much trouble with quicksands, even if we had lost some time in making detours to avoid them, but here they were so frequent that we were obliged to use flexible metal-chained rollers placed under the front wheels to ensure a better grip. Water, too, had not been a problem, except that we had often needed twice the length of rope advised in the *Michelin Guide* to bucket it up from the well. So far our journey had not been alarming but now, with the start of the hot season and with it the onset of sandstorms, conditions deteriorated, and the thousands of dead migratory birds littering the desert, their beaks and eyes blocked with sand, were a depressing sight. Only now I realised the tremendous mortality rate which migratory birds suffer. At one point we were quite frightened for a part of our engine broke and required welding. George tried to do a makeshift repair but we were stuck for the night, during which shifting sand covered our camp to a depth of several inches. This mini sandstorm made us realise how wise the authorities are to close the Sahara during the six months when such storms are a frequent occurence.

By a miracle, three Land-Rovers turned up in the morning; they were the first cars we had seen since we had entered the desert. They belonged to an American oil prospector and fortunately carried the part we needed.

As we drove north the country became rocky. Finally we reached the Berber fort of El Golea. Nearby were four towns, Ghardaia, El Ateuf, Beni Isguene and Bou Nouara, hidden among the sand hills. This is where the Moabites sought refuge in times of persecution. Here the clock seemed to have stopped some hundred years back. The people of each town lived in such strict seclusion that they did not visit each other and of course no foreign men were allowed to enter any of the towns. I had much difficulty in convincing the Berbers that I came as a friend, but I succeeded and afterwards was allowed to go in and take photographs.

During the next lap of our journey, oasis settlements became more frequent and suddenly, as if the curtain of a stage were raised, we found ourselves surrounded by an abundance of flowers and saw the Atlas Mountains in all their spring glory. The change from the bare desert to this Garden of Eden was so abrupt that I burst into tears.

We travelled on through Algiers and Morocco at a leisurely pace, camping for the sake of economy. After the meaningful emptiness of the desert, the Moorish mystics, the Catholic pomp, combined here with European culture, was overwhelming. It was easy to fall in love with Fez and Rabat, with Marrakesh – even with modern Casablanca where we said goodbye to Africa.

We then crossed via Gibraltar to Spain. We were lucky to arrive at Cadiz during the famous festival of Corpus Christi which had become a gathering of great religious and historical importance.

A few days later, in contrast, we found ourselves going down wooden ladders into deep caves. There, by the flicker of an acetylene lamp we saw engravings of mammoths very like the ones we had discovered near Lake Rudolf. At this time the Spanish caves were not open to visitors and it was only because of our description of the African engravings that an exception was made for us.

Later we visited the Alhambra. From there we saw the snow-covered peaks of the Sierra Nevada shimmering high above the clouds and this was such a challenge to us that we climbed the Veleta peak, even though we had no suitable clothes for such a venture.

Before leaving the south of Spain, a friend arranged for us to camp for a few days in the new Gredos Reserve. A guide took us on horseback into the mountains where we were able to watch closely the elusive ibex and marvel at the way in which they kept their balance when moving down precipitous cliffs. After this we went north to see more rock paintings at Altamira. I was impressed by the way in which early man expressed his aspirations by using animals as symbols.

This was really a dream world but suddenly we were shocked back to grim reality when we heard of the recent massacre at Lari by the Mau Mau. We wondered if we should not return to Kenya to help in fighting the revolt but, after exchanging several cables with our friends there, we decided to continue our trip to France.

Crossing the Pyrenees we visited Lourdes. The sight of the recurring pilgrimages of desperately ill people praying in front of the grotto, in which discarded crutches were piled along the wall, was a most impressive one. It proved how faith and will-power can succeed even where medical treatment has been defeated.

Going on to Arles, we watched there much more humane bullfights than those we had seen in Spain, for in Provence only a cockade has to be ripped off the bull's horns to achieve victory, and the animal remains unhurt.

After visiting Avignon and Carcassonne we went to see the coral fish aquarium at Monaco, a more rewarding experience than gambling in the casino. Crossing the border into Italy we climbed up to the marble quarries at Carrara. These were of special interest to me because Michelangelo and other Quattrocento sculptors had used this purest of white marble.

I wanted to show George my favourite Italian paintings, but the galleries were packed with tourists and with guides talking loudly in various languages, so the atmosphere was not a congenial one in which to enjoy masterpieces. All the same, several weeks later George suddenly remarked that the Medici Madonna in Florence was the most beautiful thing he had ever seen. My hope that he would appreciate the art and history of Europe, which was the chief cause of our visit, was plainly being fulfilled.

The Dolomites, which we crossed twice before reaching Austria, filled us with enthusiasm. In Tyrol we stayed with my friends, the Knapps, with whom I had spent many skiing holidays before I went to Kenya. We had some very happy days walking across the mountains picking edelweiss and alpen rosen which grew beside mountain brooks. George, under the guidance of my friend, climbed one of the formidable walls of the Karwendel range. We were fascinated to see chamois baby-sitting, for deep in a sheltered valley we had discovered many young kids which were being looked after by an old chamois while their mothers grazed on the higher slopes. When these returned and gave a shrill whistle the kids hopped up the scree to join them. I know many animals in Africa practise baby-sitting but so far I had not come across any European animals who did this, and it seemed to me a curious coincidence that chamois, which are the only antelope in Europe, should have baby-sitters as do their African counterparts.

After hearing a performance of *Don Giovanni* at the Salzburg Festival we went to Germany to visit Hitler's former Berghof in Berchtesgaden. By now all the buildings connected with the Nazi leaders had been destroyed, with the exception of Goebels' house which had been turned into a motel. The nearby Königsee was so crowded with tourists that it would have taken a whole day to be able to board one of the steamers that were cruising around the lake. However, by asking in English for a private boat, we obtained one within a few minutes.

On our return to Austria we drove to the glaciers of the Gross Glockner, the highest mountain in Austria, which rises to 11,483 feet.

Unfortunately, the weather was overcast when later we were at Chamonix from which we hoped to see Mont Blanc, the highest peak in the Alps (15,781 feet). The tunnel through this mountain range was being blasted for the purpose of connecting Italy with Switzerland. I wondered how long it would be before the stillness of these mountains would be spoilt by the noise of heavy traffic.

Next we drove to Vienna where my family and friends were keen to welcome George. By 1953 Vienna had recovered from the war so far as the disappearance of ruins was concerned but for me, the spirit of pre-war Vienna had gone for ever. I felt like a tourist visiting my former home.

We drove on to Switzerland via the Engadin and then to France where we 'did' all the 'musts' in Paris. By then we were so saturated with new impressions that I was glad when we reached England, where we intended to remain for some time.

We had been invited to make our HQ with friends in Norfolk. They had a lovely country house and introduced us to beagle hunts and showed us the best that East Anglian country life could offer. Later we drove to other parts of England and Scotland visiting George's friends and relations. We were fortunate to have Scotland almost to ourselves and its late autumn splendour of reddish bracken surrounding the silvery lochs. The school holidays were over and there were no tourists in sight. We even had a sunny week on the Isle of Skye, notorious for its bad weather, after which we went up to Sutherland whose beautiful, unspoiled scenery I especially enjoyed.

Whenever I mentioned having painted the Kenyan people in traditional costumes I found the subject aroused interest so I accepted an offer from *The Voice of Kenya* to arrange an English lecture tour, during which I would show slides of my paintings.

I had never lectured before and was very scared but, since all I had to do was to explain the slides, I soon got the hang of it and the lectures were very successful. On one occasion I had to address an audience of 300 women, all older than myself. When I arrived I was told that no projector was available so I was near to panic. My audience's faces looked very stern and I felt that my only way of winning them over would be to take the bull by the horns. I therefore opened my talk by saying that the circumcision rites were the most important in an African's life. The word 'circumcision' produced a hush. Nevertheless I carried on about the transformation from juvenile to adult status using the necessary sexual vocabulary as naturally as if I were talking about cooking recipes. No man was present and soon the women eased up and asked questions on a subject they had probably been brought up never to mention, but which was in fact of common interest to all of them. The lecture went very well and afterwards I was invited to tea. Stimulated by the success I had had I began to look for a publisher for a book I intended to write about the peoples of Kenya. Since this needed to be heavily illustrated and would appeal mainly to readers interested in African ethnology I would have to find a specialist publisher. I was advised to go to Sweden.

I set off in mid-January 1954. Never before had I been so far north. The light effects at this time of year were unbelievably beautiful and contrasting with the freshly fallen snow, brought out to the full the quality of the fine architecture of Stockholm.

Ake Holm met me at the airport and arranged for me to meet various interesting people and to give lectures. I had several talks with Professor Lindblom, the great anthropologist whose books I had read. I even knew his theory that wherever outriggers are found in Africa there are also masks and stilts. I had verified this curious combination when I painted the Duruma tribe, south of Mombasa on the Kenyan coast.

Unfortunately I did not find a publisher for my book so I concentrated on giving interviews and lectures to stimulate interest in the subject. Later I went to Uppsala where Ake had booked more lectures for me. I gave one in the very hall in which Linnaeus had delivered his botany specifications. I was much elated at talking from the rostrum from which this great scientist had enlightened the world with systematics which are still valid today.

Uppsala was deep in snow and everybody moved about on skis. The surroundings of the city were flat, therefore the large mounds, which were in fact Viking graves, were very popular with the skiers.

Ake took me to the weekly fur market where stacks of fox pelts competed with marten and mink skins. I was very depressed to see that thousands of these animals had been killed to provide clothes for people who could not afford woollen garments.

After a very stimulating time in Sweden I returned to England where I received a warm welcome at Kew Gardens, the British Museum and the Natural History Museum. This was in response to my having sent them collections of insects, plants and ethnographic material from Kenya. I was consulted by the authorities on which subjects would in the future be of special interest and merit research, and where such specimens could be found.

So it was with many new ideas that I sailed for Kenya. George had returned before me and had been at once involved in fighting the Mau Mau. When I arrived in Isiolo I found the windows barricaded with wire and many guards around. George helped to train a company of the Royal Inniskilling Fusiliers – our house had become their H.Q. – in tracking Mau Mau gangs trying to reach Somalia in search of arms and food. When the men were away I operated the telephone, and relayed news about gangs hiding in the hills. Since the revolt was going to be part of Kenya's history, I wished to paint a captured Mau Mau for my tribal record. Eventually I got permission to do so. Despite the heat, the man wore a heavy army great-coat, and while I painted he chatted away happily. Had I known that he was to be executed within days I could never have done his portrait. I wondered – did he know?

It took several years for independence to replace the old régime, but the transition was peaceful, and the people of Kenya worked together with the sole aim of developing their lovely country.

10

Lake Rudolf

In 1955 when the Governor, Sir Evelyn Baring, was leaving Kenya I was asked to paint a large pictorial map of the N.F.D. for him. It was designed to show the problems that had confronted him in that area and also his great interest in natural history. Sir Evelyn also wished to make a farewell safari to Lake Rudolf. George was asked to accompany him and to provide fishing tackle suitable for Nile perch, giant tilapia and tiger fish, also to advise on camping in this inhospitable region.

The most difficult problem was how to transport the flat-bottomed, fourteen-foot wooden boat with two outboard motors across the rough lava country to Loingalane, which was the only source of fresh water at the southern end of the lake.

George had always been tempted to explore South Island, but in view of the ill-fated Cambridge expedition of 1934 the authorities had absolutely forbidden him to attempt the crossing. Now, with this large boat which was so superior to our canvas dinghy, he felt he would be unable to resist the challenge.

South Island is eight miles off the mainland and is about ten miles long. It comes under the Marsabit administration, which is 180 miles away.

We planned that while George was camping with the Governor I would paint the Boran tribesmen at Marsabit. When Sir Evelyn had left I was to receive a signal to join George. So far we had kept our plans secret but when the signal arrived it went automatically to the District Officer so he had to be 'in the know'. This did no harm, for as I would be obliged to cross the eighty-miles-long Chalbi Desert, I would need his help.

Luckily the District Officer was a friend of ours and very sympathetic to our project, so he provided me with a police escort to North Horr, a tiny outpost set in a little oasis of doum palms where camels and sand grouse competed for water with the few tribal policemen.

Here Ibrahim, our loyal Somali driver, met me and leaving my car we went on in the Land-Rover. The going was very rough as we jerked from side to side between boulders or got stuck in loose sand. It made me wonder how they had managed to get a large boat over this track.

When we reached Lake Rudolf's shore an El Molo fisherman, cruising in his doum palm raft, waved a giant tilapia and then offered it to us as a present. The generosity of these very poor people is most disarming. George met us at Loingalane, where shade and the rustling of palm trees were a most welcome change from the desolate lava scenery.

George had already been near the lake for a week and had observed that every two or three days the wind changed and that this change was followed by a period of calm, which lasted up to four or five hours. He thought we might be able to cross to South Island next day during such a period.

We spent the evening preparing for the trip. We had to cut everything down to a minimum to leave room for the two outboard motors. We initially intended to use the large engine and hoped to make the crossing in an hour; if a storm arose we meant to jettison that engine and use the smaller one. Our kit included: .22 and .303 rifles, a Very pistol, rockets, ammunition, a few tools, a camera, field glasses, fishing tackle, some medicines including anti-snake-bite kit, a half-bottle of whisky for George, and finally a frying pan for cooking or bailing out. There could be no question of a change of clothes; George took a cotton loincloth and I a very thin old blanket and a toothbrush.

Next day we had to cancel our plan for the lake was churned up by a strong wind.

I painted one of the El Molo, who squatted in our tent. The island was out of reach of their log rafts and they excitedly discussed our chances of reaching it and returning safely. They told us various legends about the island; one described how, a long, long time ago, a young woman, who was pregnant, was herding her flock of goats in what is now the southern portion of the lake. She came to a spring and idly picked up a stone and started to hammer away with it at the orifice of the spring. Suddenly it burst open and a great rush of water poured out flooding the country. The young woman fled with her goats to the hills, which, surrounded by water became South Island. Here she gave birth to twins who, in course of time, peopled the island. But now there is only a terrible demon living on the island who, in the form of a goat, inhabits one of the craters. Anyone who ventures there is lured into the crater and swallowed up. Another legend tells how a family of El Molo living on the hills woke up one morning to find themselves surrounded by water. Having no boats, they were stranded and finally died out – only their goats survived. The old men among the El Molo say that their fathers told them that they used to see fires on the island, but these might have been the result of some minor volcanic activity.

The rest of the day we spent trying to make the boat un-sinkable by tying empty cans and inflated rubber tyres to it. While we were busy at our task a Land-Rover most unexpectedly appeared. In it were some reporters and the D.O. for Maralal intending to visit the El Molo. Since we had been caught red-handed we were obliged to discuss our plans, then cameras started clicking but I made the journalists promise not to publish anything till we had either returned or been drowned.

Next morning George was very anxious because if we could not make it that day he could not afford to wait any longer. The lake was covered with white horses and he became very morose. To fill in time we drove to Porr, a pyramid-shaped hill, and watched the crocodiles in the lake and the birdlife on the shore, of which there was a great deal: spoonbills, cormorants, duck, geese and sacred ibis. Next we visited the El Molo village where we received a warm welcome, the tribesmen remembering us from our last visit.

All the while George was continually looking hopefully at the lake and the island. I trusted he would not attempt the crossing and Ibrahim was of the same opinion. If, however, he did go I was determined he should not be alone.

After a time the lake began to calm down, and George then went to get the boat out. I felt very sick and retired behind a boulder to recover my courage. I scribbled a will on an old envelope and gave it to Ibrahim, asking him to hand it to the D.O. at Isiolo should I not return. Ibrahim put it in his jacket pocket and as I boarded the boat he gripped my hand and I saw that there were tears in his eyes.

George pulled furiously at the starting cord, but with no result, so for a moment I hoped that we might not set out. But suddenly, with a sound like a machine gun, the engine revved up and we were off.

I gripped the rifle and kept an eye out for crocodiles. After we had done two or three miles George shouted that he thought we would have to turn back as it was getting very rough. Nevertheless, we went on. Towards the middle of the lake we started taking in water and the flat bottom of the boat banged against the waves in a most alarming manner. However, since by then we were half-way across there was no question of our turning back.

Neither of us spoke during the hour and a quarter it took us to reach the bay we had seen from the mainland. We disembarked in a well-sheltered, sandy cove, where the water was crystal clear and teeming with fish. George got out his rod but he had no success with his spoon. I, meanwhile, investigated our immediate surroundings. The shore was inches deep in tiny pink shells and it seemed that the cove must be a crocodile maternity home, for their eggs were scattered everywhere.

We searched for a suitable camping place, safe from crocs and other menaces. We believed that if there was any game on the island the animals would probably have neither knowledge nor fear of man. The ground around was fairly well covered with *Capparis* bushes and a creeper; higher up there were cliffs of white rock and black lava.

We soon discovered that we had landed on an islet which was cut off from the main island by a channel fifty yards wide at its narrowest point. Through our glasses we scanned the coast and saw a little beach about a mile away where we thought it might be possible to land; unfortunately at the moment it was occupied by an enormous croc about twenty feet long. I was not at all anxious to seek the hospitality of such a host, but the weather was changing and we had no time to waste if we were to land before dark.

We hurried to the boat and after crossing a mile of water landed on the beach which, I was relieved to see, had been evacuated by the croc. Nevertheless, I kept a rifle handy and cast many uneasy glances at the water. The beach had a strip of sand up which we hauled the dinghy. George never shows emotion but I could see by the way in which he filled his pipe and lit it up that he was greatly elated at having at last set foot on the island.

I considered our surroundings far from inviting. Directly behind us and on either side were jagged lava flows, but we had no time to study the scenery. What we needed to do was to find a sheltered place in which we could spend the night. We chose a cleft in an isolated rock near the beach. It was just long enough and wide enough to harbour the two of us lying head to tail. We pushed most of our possessions in with us, weighting everything down with stones for fear it might blow away. Then we cleared away bits of the larger lava so that we could lie on the pebbles that covered the ground. While we were busy with this task the headlights of the Land-Rover showed across the lake. George fired a Very light in reply. The headlights of the car replied three times, then followed a firework display of .303 tracer bullets. Evidently the men were pleased that we had arrived safely.

George had made careful arrangements with Ibrahim about signals: one Very light meant 'all well', three 'we have run out of food', five 'we need to be rescued'. In the last two cases Ibrahim was to drive to North Horr and also get in touch by radio with Marsabit.

When night fell I pulled up my thin blanket and George wrapped himself in his *kikoi*. We pretended to be comfortable but whenever I turned I was reminded that I was lying on pebbles, it is true not on sharp lava, but still pebbles are pebbles. Then the gale started up, gusts tore across the lake and shot through our cleft in ice-cold blasts, which had a terrifying force. There was no hope of sleep, all we could do was to wait for dawn, and it was a long wait. Well before sunrise we got up, made a fire and brewed tea. At sunrise we saw waves tossing wildly against the lava and sending up spray twenty feet high. Not long afterwards we observed the Land-Rover's lights across the water and plainly faithful Ibrahim wanted to make sure that we had not been swallowed up by the demon during the night.

After a breakfast of bully beef we packed some dates and some biscuits and started to climb up the ridge. The going was very tiring, often dangerous. We kept to the edge of the lava flows, trying to avoid fissures and picking our way across pastry-thin pieces of hollow-sounding lava. Sometimes it gave way beneath our feet and we had to jump to the next safe foot-hold. Climbing over pinnacles of jagged lava and up the irregular surfaces of the brittle flows was no easy task. Fortunately, the highest slopes where clinker and cinders replaced lava were easier going. Reaching a saddle I saw a succession of craters along the skyline. George pointed to a small herd of goats; they looked like the common native goat and in spite of the meagre grazing seemed to be in excellent condition. I began to wonder whether there might be some truth in the El Molo legends.

At the top of the first crater we reached, we found a cairn, evidently erected by Dyson and Martin, members of the Fuchs expedition in 1934, who were drowned here. The wind was unpleasant and we did not linger but I collected some plants: a portulaca and a woody herb which I put in my collecting bag.

On our way to the highest peak we passed through a little valley covered in dried-up vegetation, mostly frankincense trees. These grow very slowly and it was difficult to understand how they had succeeded in maturing where other vegetation had hardly got a hold.

Near the summit the wind was so strong that several times I was literally blown over. It needed a lot of determination to breast its fury, but we reached the top and found that our efforts had been well worth while, for a magnificent view of nearly the whole of the island lay spread out before us. Three phases of volcanic action could be seen. Several major volcanoes had erupted their lava to the east in steep, red flows that fell into the lake. This was the face we had climbed. The most recent eruption appeared to have taken place at the northern end of the island, where yellowish tuff was overlaid with jet-black flows. The western side presented a very different picture: it consisted of gently undulating hills, scantily covered with bush, and along the shore there were beaches and excellent landing places.

The crater immediately below us was covered with dried-up frankincense trees. Here we saw another cairn and several more by distant craters. We now built our own cairn and then began the difficult descent. This was particularly unpleasant for George who was wearing sandals. We took the shortest route to be in time for the evening signal.

The lake had not calmed down so there was no question of being able to fish for our supper. We heated up a tin of bully beef and improved our sleeping quarters by building walls of stones at either end of the cleft to protect us from the icy blast. The wind was blowing with increasing violence and this night seemed even longer than the previous one, but I forgot all my discomforts when George appeared in the early morning with a giant tilapia which he had shot. He is a good cook and we had a delicious breakfast; after which, filled with enthusiasm, we started for the southern end of the island, hoping to find Dyson's and Martin's camp.

We passed several creeks swarming with crocs which glided into the lake at our approach – this surprised us for why should they be so shy when on the island they could never have known human enemies? It made me wonder whether they had been bred on the mainland; anyway I was glad of their show of respect.

When we reached the channel from which we had landed, we stood bewildered at the number of crocs, averaging sixteen to eighteen feet in length; surprised, too, that the tilapia swam among them apparently unconcerned. We looked for the long-snouted croc which is said to inhabit the lake but saw only the common variety.

Suddenly we caught sight of another herd of goats; George stalked and photographed them.

We continued our way along the coast and found the going

even worse than the previous day's climb. This was because we had to cross the lava flows instead of walking along the ridges; on our way, we met more goats who seemed to thrive on the coarse spiky grass that grew along the shore.

Of Dyson's and Martin's camp we saw no sign, but we were not surprised at this for it was impossible to imagine anyone landing on this inhospitable coast unless forced to do so. All around were cast skins of snakes, and this alarmed me considerably until George assured me that they belonged to the apparently harmless striped sand snake, of which we had seen some live ones. I looked for fossils, but in vain. All we found were bones of a giraffe and hippo; no doubt they had been washed up from the mainland.

When we returned to our cleft we found the lake still too rough for fishing and ate our last tin of bully beef. All the same, it was pleasant to sit and enjoy a sun-downer, even if it had to be mixed with brackish water that turned everything a yellowish green, for we were surrounded by unbelievably beautiful scenery. Our immediate background was a stark mass of towering lava, which had fallen from the rims of the volcanoes, covering everything in its path. There was little life to be seen, except for the cruising crocs, a reminder of life only in the shed snake skins, and real warm blooded life in the goats, to whom my heart went out.

We were faced by an overpowering majesty of nature, her glory enhanced by isolation and the knowledge that the wild gales would discourage any frivolous invasion of our solitude.

Who has not dreamed of living on a desert island, or of living like Adam and Eve? For us, this dream had come true, we were the only familiar and friendly beings here, each utterly dependent on the other and continually surrounded by danger.

But during all the time I spent on the island I was never able to rid myself of a strange feeling of fear. Fear of the deadness around us, fear that George fishing from a slippery rock might fall into the sea and be taken by a croc, fear that one of us might crash down into a fissure of the lava, fear of the return crossing – more dangerous than the outward journey because we would be going against the wind.

Never before had I been so conscious of how precious life is; not just our own lives but the lives around us. Until now I had always taken it for granted that I would wake to bird song and my first glance would rest on trees and flowers – wake to things as alive as I was myself. But now we were trapped by the gale on this island of death, while the merciless sun sapped our endurance.

The third night was even worse than its predecessors and I relaxed only when dawn broke. I called to George; there was no reply. What could have happened? In a panic I climbed a hill behind our camp but could see no sign of him. I kept on saying to myself that he must be fishing, then I turned back and found some fragments of local pottery with crude ornamentation on them. For a moment this distracted me from my anxiety but once I had packed up these finds for the museum, fear returned. To kill time I inspected our anti-snake-bite outfit and wrote up my diary. Two hours passed. Then, to my joy, George appeared carrying a baby croc and a tilapia. We certainly had an excellent breakfast but I made George promise that never again would he disappear without warning me.

After lunch we skinned the croc and mended our tattered shoes, then we went to look for fuel. This search occupied the whole day.

Following what might be described as a rough path, just above the high-water mark, we came upon a small stone wall, a few feet long. Who had built it and for what purpose? In the vicinity we found more fragments of pottery which we collected to compare with others I had got on the mainland.

When we returned to our cleft George fished and I felt very nervous as I saw him slip about on the wet, slimy rocks. In the end he shot a tilapia and the shock of the bullet stunned two little fish. They were two inches long, deep-red with iridescent green markings on their fins. While we were examining them a cobra suddenly reared and spat at George; fortunately it was too far off for the venom to reach his eyes. I pointed out that my fear of poisonous snakes had not been without foundation. George confessed that that very morning he had killed a small spitting cobra in my make-shift bed.

Later in the day George gave an exclamation – under a heap of stones he had found an empty whisky bottle and a few rusty sardine tins. Obviously Dyson and Martin had used the exact site we had chosen and being tidy people had buried their camp litter before setting out on their fatal journey.

After another cold and sleepless night, morning brought little hope of calmer weather, so we decided to explore the northern end of the island. We followed a rough track until it faded out, after which we had to pick our way over broken lava. Many crocs slid into the water at our approach. After three hours we came to a wide bay with a pebbly beach which would make an excellent landing place. At the old lake level, some fifteen feet above the present water-line, we saw, amongst other debris, a round four-gallon petrol drum and a length of red inner tube. These, we felt sure, were wreckage from Dyson's and Martin's boat for they had used two such drums for buoyancy. At this point I decided to leave a copy of my diary behind since it could be of use to future explorers if we met with disaster.

A fifteen-foot wall of lava blocked one end of the bay, we climbed over it and then crossed several recent flows: they were black whilst the older lava was red. The most northerly crater was mainly tuff, in which we found oysters and other shells. They were the only signs of prehistoric life we had seen on the island, though on the mainland opposite there were plenty of fossils. From the rim of this crater we had a fine view, to the west was an open bay with a perfect landing place. We did not see any cairns on the northern volcanoes. On the north coast where the cliff fell precipitously into deep water, we were astonished to see thousands of big tilapia, many with their backs out of the water, gnawing hungrily at a pink deposit which covered the rocks. Further out were large shoals of fish, packed so closely together that they looked like dark clouds. We wondered whether they might have come there to breed.

As the wind was dropping George suggested that we should hurry back in case there might be a chance of our making the return journey. We were anxious to leave as soon as possible for our provisions were very low and our footwear had just about had it. But no sooner had we got back to our camp than the wind got up and dashed our hopes. We passed the time collecting goat skulls, snake skins, beetles, centipedes, lizards, plants and little red fish – all of which we packed up in our empty tins.

We had now been prisoners of the island for seven days and I began to wonder whether the wind ever dropped. I could imagine Dyson and Martin becoming as impatient as I was and then deciding to risk the crossing, with fatal results.

I had little sleep that night so towards luncheon time I decided to take a siesta. From this I was woken by the sound of a boat being dragged down the beach and realised that George was preparing for our crossing. Certainly the lake was now much calmer. In less than fifteen minutes all was ready and George pulled the cord, but the engine was obstinate and refused to start, so he plunged waist-deep into the water to try to discover the cause. At that moment I noticed a croc swimming very near him but before I could shout, the engine had revved up, he had leapt on board and we were off.

I was very uneasy and sitting rigid in the bows, gripped my rifle and concentrated my thoughts on crocs. When we were a mile out the lake became very rough and we began to toss about alarmingly; George suggested that it might be better if we returned, I did not reply and we went on; but after another mile we turned round. Back on the island I started to mend my shoes and to pack two croc skulls that I had forgotten. Later in the afternoon the whitecaps disappeared, the lake became calmer and we realised that we had just time to cross before dark. We started off again.

The lake may have looked calm but it was not long before I was obliged to start bailing with the frying pan, and it was not until we were near the mainland that I felt able to relax. At that moment the engine spluttered and died. I seized the oars and began rowing. George cursed the outboard engine but a minute later discovered that we had merely run out of petrol. Since we had a reserve supply we soon got going again. Now we saw two figures on the shore and I started to cry with relief. As we neared the beach the men waded into the lake to meet us. They told us that in the early morning they had walked to this spot. When I asked them how they knew that we would come today they told me that a Rendile girl, gifted with second sight, had said that we would return on this day. I was touched when they told me that during our absence all in the camp were in such a state of tension that no one liked to look another in the eyes.

It was not long before our car arrived to give the evening signal. Ibrahim was wild with delight when he knew that we were safely back. As soon as we reached camp, the El Molo appeared from nowhere and bombarded us with questions. Finally, the chief told us that he meant to settle on this island paradise with all his people and take possession of the goats, which we thought might number about two hundred.

The next morning I was woken by the noise of an aircraft, which circled low over the camp and dropped two packets of cigarettes and a message which read:

Delighted to see you safe, will send the news everywhere. Yours very cheered . . .
P.S. with the compliments of K.P.R. Air Wing

A few hours later we were at North Horr, where we found two Europeans who had come up from Marsabit and were about to set out to rescue us. Not long afterwards five police officers arrived bent on the same task.

The way in which our secret had leaked out was this: George was expected at an important meeting in Nairobi – when he failed to turn up enquiries were made. There was anxiety for our safety and the District Commissioners of Marsabit and Maralal felt obliged to disclose our intention of going to South Island. Hearing this, the authorities were so alarmed that the P.C. of Isiolo immediately booked two graves in the Nyeri Cemetery.

Later we were summoned to his office and he began by reprimanding George for disobeying orders and costing the administration a lot of money mounting rescue teams, but in the end he said, with a smile, how proud he was of our achievement and how much he wished he had been with us.

All we had to offer as a result of our expedition were some facts about South Island, mostly negative: the lack of wild life except allowed them to grow up wild, whilst accepting us as their foster parents. The latter was due to 'imprinting' – the term used to describe the fact that any newly born animal is apt to regard the first creature it sees on opening its eyes as its mother. We called the cubs Lustica, The Big One and Elsa; all were females. Elsa, though the runt of the family, was the bravest and the most lovable. After the trio became too big for us to keep them unrestrained, we presented Lustica and The Big One to the Rotterdam Zoo, while Elsa continued living free with us.

When she became mature we moved her to a remote area in the Meru Park, hoping that here we could rehabilitate her to a completely wild life. We were prepared to do this, even if it meant the end of our relationship with her. But it never came to that as Elsa learned to be independent but still retained her love and loyalty for us. This experiment was so successful that eventually she mated with a wild lion.

At this point we felt that we should share our experiences by writing a book and thus stimulate interest in wild animals at a time when they were so much in need of help.

George had no time for writing and I felt too inexperienced to make a book based on my notes, so, I suggested to Elspeth Huxley that she might undertake the task. Her reply was that the book must be written in the first person. I therefore began to write.

Lord William Percy, who had known Elsa since she was a tiny cub, gave me a lot of good advice, stressing that I should neither be anthropomorphic about Elsa, nor describe her behaviour as though it were due solely to conditioned reflexes and release mechanisms, thus denying her intelligence, reasoning and feeling. It was also he who suggested the title *Born Free* to me.

When I had finished the text, I went to England and gave myself a month to find a publisher. My first attempts were unsuccessful. When my time was running out, I happened to remember a correspondence I had had with Mrs Villiers of the Harvill Press about a book on the tribes of Kenya which I intended writing. She had replied that the project sounded to her more suitable to a university press than to her firm. On a cold and rainy day I happened to pass the office of the Harvill Press, so I rang the bell and asked to see Mrs Villiers. I reminded her of my plan to write a book about the tribes of Kenya, but then told her that the manuscript I was now offering was something quite different. She asked me to tell her the story. I did so and she was obviously impressed. I told her that I had hundreds of photographs of Elsa and she suggested that her partner, Mrs Harari, should come to my flat and look at them, as she was particularly concerned with illustrations. By that evening both had expressed great interest in my book but neither had made an offer, so next day I went to see an agent. In fact, while I was doing this Mrs Villiers had cabled to the Chairman of William Collins, who was abroad at that time, telling him that my book sounded to her like a bestseller and that it was essential to make a good offer for it at once since I was in touch with other publishers. Subsequently I learned that the Harvill Press was a subsidiary of Collins.

Immediately after his return Billy Collins, Mrs Villiers and Mrs Harari met me at his office. His was a strong personality with great charm, but he merely glanced at my photographs and at the text, remarking that he might consider publication but only after consulting with his board. I left the meeting no wiser than when I had entered.

It was not long, however, before I was offered a contract and an advance of £1,000. I was in doubt as to whether this was a good proposition or not, so again I consulted Elspeth Huxley, who strongly advised me to accept.

Collins have an outstanding promotion and distribution organisation, and before the day of publication huge posters drawing the attention of Londoners to *Born Free* and life-size models of Elsa were displayed in bookshops. Collins had been prepared for a big sale, but in the event the number sold far exceeded all expectation. Within a short time the book had been translated into twenty-five languages.

When I returned to Kenya I found that Elsa had borne three cubs. After their birth she disappeared for six weeks. Then quite unexpectedly there she was on the other side of the river from our camp. Very soon the whole family swam over to visit us. I restrained myself from touching them for fear they might become imprinted on me, but in fact Elsa had probably avoided this from happening by keeping the cubs away from us for six weeks.

Elsa

Pippa

An experiment performed in the United States has proved that in the case of a puppy, during the first nineteen days it is virtually unconscious – just eating, digesting and sleeping, but on the nineteenth day something seems to click and from then onwards the puppy becomes aware of being a dog and reacts accordingly. Other animals click into self-awareness at different periods. From Elsa we learned that for lions the period is six weeks as she had kept her cubs from us till they had established their identity.

For the next two years Elsa acted as liaison between her family and ourselves. The cubs regarded us as their mother's friends but never allowed us to become familiar with them. During this time we kept all our visitors away so that the young lions should be able to live completely wild when we withdrew. The life span of a wild lion is twelve to fifteen years, but when Elsa was five years old and the cubs seventeen months she became ill, and after a few days she died. The post mortem showed that she had a tick infection which had destroyed her red blood corpuscles. The disease known as *Babesia felis* had hitherto been unknown amongst lions. My relationship with Elsa had not only widened my understanding of animal behaviour and psychology; it had introduced me to a world denied to most human beings. With Elsa's death a vital part of myself died too.

Another chapter of our lives opened when we found ourselves the guardians of Elsa's cubs who were not yet quite old enough to hunt for themselves. Worse still, a lioness who had originally occupied the territory in which they were living, asserted her rights once Elsa was dead and drove the cubs out. There followed a long and anxious search for them, and when we did find them we were obliged to capture them in very difficult circumstances and take them to the Serengeti National Park in Tanzania where they could be returned to the wild. I have told their story in *Living Free* and *Forever Free*.

I had been warned in advance that I would have to pay a high rate of tax on my royalties. I therefore decided to make over all the income to a tax-free charitable organisation to help wild animals in their struggle for survival. This had become a world-wide problem and if drastic action were not taken soon wild animals might be exterminated. We human beings seem to have forgotten that we have no right to live at the expense of other creatures. In doing this we are also jeopardising our own future, for no species can survive in isolation, together we depend on ecology – the cooperation of all creatures and all organic matter in maintaining life.

The unbelievable impact Elsa had on readers of all ages and nations made me wonder if she had not been sent to us at this crucial time to make us conscious again of a world we had almost lost, a world in which we were still a part of nature and lived in harmony with other creatures. Reading about Elsa, people seemed to realise how empty our lives would be without animals and how lovable they could be if only we allowed them to be themselves and did not treat them as inferior, dumb and stupid. Elsa was rapidly winning the hearts of people all over the world and, judging from her fan mail, she had changed the philosophies and careers of many of her readers who suddenly became aware of the basic values of life. Meanwhile the exploitation and destruction of wild animals went on. Hoping to improve the situation, in 1969 I launched the Elsa Wild Animal Appeal in England. A board of trustees in London controlled all the funds; it was assisted by an advisory committee in Kenya which recommended priorities.

Meanwhile, soon after the publication of *Forever Free*, Collins organised a worldwide tour for me. For this I used a film which George and I had shot while sharing Elsa's life. We had made it purely for our own pleasure, so there was no trick photography or forced action. All it needed was professional editing. There were some very moving scenes in it and as I write these lines nearly a quarter of a century later, the film is still running in libraries and schools.

My first public appearance was in London before an audience of 3,000 people. The night before I was so scared that I was actually sick. Though I had spoken English since I was a child, I had an Austrian accent and my vocabulary was far from perfect. I therefore took elocution lessons, both to improve my English and also to try to slow down my speech, for my thoughts always run ahead of my words. I was not successful in this exercise so in the end we arranged that my tutor would sit in the front row and raise a little red flag when I should put the brakes on.

How varied my audiences were can be illustrated by a day in London when, in the morning, I lectured to businessmen. I had assumed that they were chiefly interested in trade, but as soon as I heard their questions and comments I realised how deeply involved many of them were in natural history. At luncheon time I gave a lecture to the women in Holloway Prison. So many came that we had to use the chapel, it being the largest room, and I spoke from the pulpit. In the front rows sat the minor offenders, shoplifters, prostitutes and so on; the serious criminals were seated at the back. Before I started to speak there were whistles and catcalls, but once I had begun my lecture there was silence until the end, then bedlam broke out and there were constant shouts of 'Elsa, Elsa!', while the women searched their pockets for the few pennies they were allowed to spend on cigarettes and sweets. Their offerings for the Elsa Fund nearly burned my hands for I realised that the donors were depriving themselves of their few luxuries in order to help endangered animals. When later I visited men's prisons I met with the same reaction. All this made me aware that in most of these prisoners who found it difficult, if not impossible, to loosen up in front of people, a love of nature and of the animal world was deeply buried. It made me wonder why many of us remain on guard with other human beings while in the presence of animals we can relax and be at our best. Might this be due to our more evolved intellect which separates us and makes us more critical of each other while animals iron out our differences and give us a harmony which we seldom give each other?

Later, on this same day, I went to Kensington Palace to show the film to Princess Marina, Duchess of Kent. She had a most charming personality and I felt completely at ease with her for she was deeply interested in Elsa and in Kenyan wildlife. The butler poured out tea and set the film going. I should have enjoyed it more had I not been aware that the Princess's Pekingese had discovered the long gloves I had arrived in, to conform to court etiquette, and was busy gnawing them to shreds.

After lecturing in England I toured the world. In South

Africa I was flown for two days to the Kruger National Park, where I realised that the most pressing problem was to limit the ever-increasing number of visitors. The animals kept clear of the never-ending convoys of cars along the dusty roads and, consequently, became more and more difficult to see. To compensate for this disappointment, football and other entertainments were provided for the tourists.

During a drive around the park we came on some fifty stationary cars, we parked ours nearby, with little hope of seeing any animals. Suddenly, to our astonishment, an old and a young lion came into view and dodging between the cars stopped right in front of us to settle their rival leadership of the pride.

They sprang at each other, tearing at the rival's mane, locking their jaws and striking out with their paws, till we thought that we heard their bones crack – and all this was happening within a few yards of our car. Breathing heavily and giving deep growls, the two rolled over and over until the older lion became exhausted and exposed his belly as a sign of surrender. This put an immediate end to the fight. The old lion, limping badly, went off into a thicket, while the young lion, licking his wounds, turned in the opposite direction. The press photographer who had been seconded to me took many photographs of the contest which, according to the park authorities, was the first ever to be witnessed here.

Before I left I had the privilege of meeting one of the two men who had created the park; Spice Wollhuter was then very old and bedridden. In his youth he had stabbed a lion to death single-handed, with a small knife.

One evening I lectured in Cape Town and afterwards there followed an autograph-signing session. I was by then very tired so I simply wrote my name down without even looking up. Later I discovered that amongst the autograph hunters was my first husband, Ziebel von Klarwill – he had pocketed my signature without comment.

In Port Elizabeth I saw the famous snake research station which provided the anti-snake-bite serum on which we relied in Kenya. I was also invited to see the porpoises in the aquarium. I was interested to learn that, like lions and elephants, they have aunts who act as baby-sitters and also have foster mothers ready to take care of the infants should they lose their real mother. One enchanting porpoise did complicated acrobatics at the request of her keeper. It was obvious that they were very fond of each other. Later the keeper tried to induce the porpoise to allow me to touch her. She made it clear that she did not care for such a degree of intimacy with a stranger, but in the end, just to please her friend, she obliged; swam up to me, winced when I touched her silky head and then was off to the other end of the pool.

On leaving South Africa I flew to New Delhi, Thailand and Singapore – then on to Australia. In the course of this journey I was interested to discover what a strong influence the zodiac still has on the Chinese. One manifestation of it is that people born under the sign of the tiger or of the lion – the most unlucky of all signs – often fake their birth certificates in order to avoid the disastrous consequences they anticipate. This made me study the influence which animals have had, from the time of cavemen to the present day, on the emblems of religion, history and heraldry. Later I used such examples in my lectures and illustrated the fact that animals often symbolise many of our aspirations.

In Singapore I even felt ashamed that I was a human being. The guide told me that if I paid him £1 extra I could have a 'special treat'. I did so and was conducted to the house of communal wailing, where the poorest of the poor, who had no private place in which they could perform the mourning rites demanded by the Chinese religion, spent the last hours with those they loved in company with equally poor mourning families. When I realised that this was my 'special treat' I left at once, appalled that anyone could make money by letting tourists pry into private grief as a form of entertainment.

In Australia I lectured in Perth, Adelaide, Melbourne, Sydney and Brisbane. Except for a few, small wildlife parks close to these cities there were then no animal reserves in the coastal hinterland where rapid development had deprived the local animals of their territory. If they tried to return to it they were shot down. There was no control. I was also unhappy about the conditions which then existed in most zoos. The enclosures were inadequate –

gregarious animals were isolated and solitary animals were put together. It was evident that a study of natural animal behaviour was lacking. When I lunched with the Governor-General at Canberra I pleaded for the establishment of National Parks, to which Australia's unique marsupials would certainly attract many visitors.

While in Melbourne I stayed with friends who took me to a forest-clad mountain, where lyre-birds live. We drove thirty miles through heavy rain and then entered the dripping forest. Soon we heard the unmistakable call of this rare bird and followed the sound into a thicket, where we saw a lyre-bird displaying its exquisite tail feathers in the shape of a half-circle. It took three steps to the right, then burst into song, then three steps to the left, and repeated this performance many times. At first the bird had its back to us, then it turned and faced us and continued with its dance and vocalisation. We were lucky to witness this display, for the lyre-bird is very difficult to see and few people have the opportunity of doing so.

In Brisbane I saw my first platypus. He lived in a little stream but had to be confined because the spur on his hindlegs contained a deadly poison during the breeding season, and he could be dangerous when alarmed. This was demonstrated by holding a washing-mop near him. Instantly the platypus attacked this intruder in his territory with all the fury with which he would attack an enemy, injecting the venom repeatedly into the mop.

My Australian tour was packed full and very tiring. In the end I left for New Zealand on a stretcher.

When I arrived at Auckland airport a press conference awaited me and also a doctor, whom the representative of Collins in New Zealand had asked to give me a check-up. He cancelled my public appearances and insisted on my taking a rest.

New Zealand has some of the most beautiful scenery in the world and now I had a chance to appreciate it. One of the Collins local managers drove me to the Bay of Islands. It is a sparsely inhabited region in the extreme north and I was not booked to give any lectures there. I found myself in a dream land of un-believable peace and beauty, and spent a wonderful week beachcombing in the sun; by then I felt completely relaxed and fit to go back to public life.

While buying petrol in a tiny village which had only one general store, I was touched when the owner produced a copy of *Born Free* and asked me to autograph it. The book had obviously been much read and since the man had no advance knowledge that we would call on him, I knew that this was not a publicity stunt.

My first lecture was to be in the south of South Island. We flew there in a small plane through a snowstorm. It was such a bouncy flight that for the only time in my life I was air-sick. The pilot was obliged to make an emergency landing and when I arrived, bedraggled, at Invercargill I was several hours late for the lecture. At first my reception was frosty but when the audience realised that it was a near-miracle that I had arrived at all, they gave me an enthusiastic welcome.

While at Christchurch I was invited to spend a weekend at a skiing hut, high up in the mountains. I also visited the Hermitage, South Island's famous luxury resort. Later I flew on to the Mount Cook glacier where I could see the routes on which Sir Edmund Hillary had practised for his conquest of Mount Everest.

I had been told that New Zealanders were extremely interested in wildlife and wondered whether this might be partly because of the absence of indigenous animals, except for the kiwi and other flightless birds, and the tuatara, a prehistoric lizard dating back 400 million years which is as cold to the touch as if it had just come out of a deep freezer. The Emperor Franz Joseph sent deer and chamois to South Island but he omitted to send predators with them, with the result that they over-bred and have become such a pest that a bounty is offered for killing them. Trigger-happy youngsters go out shooting but fail to follow up the wounded beasts. The Society for the Prevention of Cruelty to Animals has intervened, as they did also with people who tethered their sheepdogs to small shelters on the borders of sheep farms and often left them without food or water for many days. While in New Zealand I spoke about these cruelties and was made an honorary member of the S.P.C.A. The warm response that my talks received in New Zealand made lecturing there a pleasure.

On my way to the United States I spent Christmas Eve in Fiji. It is an enchanting island, the air heavy with the scent of flowers which on that evening competed with the aromatic smell of delicious Fijian food simmering in earthenware pots, around which the people danced in colourful costumes against a background of glistening palm fronds and a moon-lit ocean.

On my flight to Honolulu I crossed the date line and thus had another, though very different, Christmas celebration. The place was so full of tourists that it was impossible to find a space on the beach, or for that matter, a seat at a table in my five-star hotel. After walking round for hours I ended up in a milk bar, where I had an ice-cream for my Christmas dinner.

While in Honolulu I visited the zoo and made friends with the Director. He had made his zoo interesting by grouping together animals who live in a similar habitat and would in the wild share the same water-hole. The day I was due to fly to San Francisco he took me to a view-point from which I could photograph geysers in the ocean. I took my handbag with me and my camera. To get a closer view we left the car and walked some twenty yards towards the sea. I heard another car stop for a moment and then go on but I was too busy taking photographs to pay any attention to this. When I returned to change my film I found that my handbag had gone and with it my passport, traveller's cheques, air tickets, insurance, my diary and letters of introduction, as well as the manuscript of a new book, on which I had been working during my flights. We instantly informed the police, who said that I had undoubtedly been the victim of a gang of thieves who used children playing round the cars to grab the loot. Despite strenuous efforts on the part of the police the thieves could not be traced. The Director of the zoo kindly lent me money and got me a seat on a plane. Luckily, I was already in United States territory; this was indeed fortunate for it was a whole year before my passport was renewed.

Meanwhile, when the agency which was organising my lectures in the United States heard that I had already spent six

Elsamere, view of Lake Naivasha

One of its visitors – a Goliath heron

Colobus monkeys

months lecturing, they trebled their insurance on me. Given the schedule prepared for me I could understand why they thought I might become ill. Not only was I to give three lectures every day for the next six months, but I had breakfast, lunch and dinner interviews, broadcasts and TV programmes and signing sessions as well. Nevertheless, as soon as it was realised how popular Elsa was, disregarding the long flights involved, every spare hour was filled with still more lectures. Thus one morning I would find myself talking to an audience in Maine, lunching in North Carolina and in the evening speaking in Chicago.

By then I had unknowingly developed a rigid posture during public performances, restricting the movements of my hands to the minimum. This was an instinctive defence reaction to help prevent me from breaking down when I was asked morbid questions about Elsa. Her death had affected me deeply and I had never been given time to recover – on the contrary, I had been plunged into a life in which I had to talk constantly about her and show the film of her three times a day. The more emotional I felt, the more I stood stiff like a statue, afraid that the slightest movements might loosen my self-control. I was asked by several psychiatrists how I could stand the strain, but I had no alternative. However hard I tried to vary my lectures, I had to repeat the same stories and this sometimes made me feel I was going mad.

My schedule often sapped my vitality to such an extent that I walked on to the platform not knowing how I would start, let alone get through the lecture. Yet once I faced the audience it was as if my talk were dictated by an unknown power. I felt like an outsider, detached and listening to myself. I wondered whether I had become simply a medium for conveying Elsa's message. In the past, watching her, I had realised that animals are able to communicate over hundreds of miles and also to impose orders which stand for several days. This made me question the possibility that what I was now experiencing was some sort of extra-sensory perception. However, I kept these ideas to myself since I did not wish to be regarded as a crank.

While I was rushing madly from Fifth Avenue to Third Avenue, trying to glimpse the sky above the concrete chasms of New York's skyscrapers and almost deafened by the noise of traffic, I was thinking of Kenya, of its vast uninhabited spaces, of its tranquillity, of its varied and magnificent animals who at that moment were making their way to familiar water-holes. I longed to return to their peaceful world.

When I finally went back to Kenya it was to help in the shooting of Columbia's film production of *Born Free*. Contrary to precedent, even though I was the author, I was asked to live on location and vouch for the fair treatment of the animals involved, give interviews to the various societies for the prevention of cruelty to animals whose representatives visited us, write articles about the film and brief the press.

The location was a 700-acre farm near Nanyuki at the foot of Mount Kenya. The farmhouse was used by us for sleeping and social activities, extensive sleeping quarters had been built for the crew of sixty, and tents were set up for the trainers who looked after the twenty-four lions, the elephants and other animals. To accommodate some hundred African labourers, a small village was established nearby.

Columbia had hired two circus lionesses, with their trainers, to act the part of Elsa but when Virginia McKenna and Bill Travers, who were taking the lead parts, were confronted with these plump cats they refused to work with them because each of their movements had to be controlled by the trainers and it was obvious that the deep affection which had existed between Elsa and ourselves could never be conveyed. The Traverses insisted that they should be allowed two months before the filming started to make friends with a couple of half-grown cubs – Boy and Girl – only in this way could they establish a relationship similar to the one we had enjoyed with Elsa. The producer agreed. Under George's guidance they all played football on the adjoining plains, chased balloons, clambered up trees, picnicked together and had a wonderful time, until the cubs had become as friendly and cooperative as they needed to be for acting the role of Elsa.

During one of their romps George got tired and rested on the grass flat out on his stomach. Girl spotted him and stalked him in proper feline fashion. With her belly close to the ground, she made a crouching approach, finally rushing forward to bite him in the neck. We watched terrified as it had happened too quickly for us to intervene. What was our relief when, having put her muzzle on George's neck, the cub sat down quietly, waiting for him to get up and pat her. (Evidently she could not control her natural instinct to hunt a prey unconscious of her presence, but when it came to the final killing, she seemed to know that this was her friend whom she must not hurt.) This hunting game became a daily habit, not only between George and Girl, but also with two other stand-by lionesses. Thus, if the script demanded that a lioness should walk in a straight line to a certain point and nothing would induce her to do so, all we had to do was to use George as a bait concealed from the cameras.

A tricky fighting scene between Elsa and her rival lioness was made possible by using the territorial instinct of lions, who will ruthlessly chase any intruder off their ground. To prepare the right setting, a large rocky outcrop was fenced in around its base in which two lionesses were confined but strictly separated, so that they never met each other. They were fed on a rocky platform on the top of the hill – one in the morning, one in the late afternoon. As soon as both seemed to claim their territorial right to this rock, they were fed at the same time. Instantly, they charged each other with wide-open fangs, biting and clawing and rolling over in a fight which never could have been staged. To prevent possible injuries, the fire brigade from Nanyuki had previously installed four large water tanks and were ready to drench the lionesses to part them. Luckily this was not needed as the fight stopped when both animals were too exhausted to continue and could safely be led to their quarters.

This scene alone should have earned *Born Free* an Oscar, but since this new approach to dealing with dangerous animals in a film was unknown to the judges, *Born Free* won the Oscar only for its music. It had however a worldwide success following its Royal Première in London at which the Queen was present.

12

My Cheetah
and
a House in Naivasha

During the filming of *Born Free*, while I was living on the film location, an army officer offered me a young female cheetah for rehabilitation. Half a year before, he had found the cub apparently abandoned and had reared her as a pet with his children. Now he was being transferred to Europe and did not wish to expose the cub to a cold climate. This is how Pippa came into my life.

We made a spacious wire enclosure, from which she could see me and I took her for walks on a leash and played with her in all my spare time. Whenever we passed the lion enclosure I had to keep her under very strict control, to prevent her from panicking, for lions and cheetahs are natural enemies. Once past the lions, I often let her roam around chasing birds and antelope on the neighbouring plains. Her killing instinct had not yet developed and she never harmed any of the creatures, but these games helped to arouse her hunting instinct. In cats the instinct to kill develops surprisingly late. Elsa was seventeen months old before she tried to kill and twenty-two months before she did it efficiently. Cheetahs kill at fourteen months but remain dependent on their mother for hunting for another three or four months. Only then can they fend for themselves.

On the other hand, from birth all cats know how to drag a kill and, when stalking, how to take advantage of the direction of

One of the cubs, Elsa, was to become world famous

George and Joy with Elsa

Elsa bringing her 3 cubs to our camp

At Elsa's camp: Billy Collins with George Adamson

Juliette and Julian Huxley

At the Royal Command Performance of *Born Free*, London, 1966

Malcolm MacDonald, on the right, hosting a luncheon at Government House for Mzee Jomo Kenyatta, his daughter Margaret, his future Vice President Murumbi with Carl Foreman in centre, Bill Travers with Virginia McKenna at left next to Joy, and two future ministers. Nairobi, 1964

Pippa with Joy

Pippa took me to see her cubs

Tatu and Whity

The story of Elsa has reached millions of people

the wind. Later I took Pippa to the Meru Park with the sole aim of returning a spoilt pet to wild life, I did not then imagine that she would lead me into a new and enchanting world; lions are gregarious and, as such, easy to understand; cheetahs are solitary and enigmatic. Their best defence is not their famous speed but their capacity to conceal themselves. Elsa and Pippa dominated my life for ten years but they were so totally different that they were more like friends who complemented each other, rather than rivals for my affection. While Elsa used our camp as her home and brought her cubs there to see us, Pippa preferred to live a few miles away and if we wanted to share her life we had to visit her. I was glad to see that her years as a pet had done nothing to impair her natural instincts. As soon as she was mature she searched for a mate; we never saw him, but until she became pregnant we used to see his spoor.

Tragically, Pippa's first four cubs were killed by lions. She lost no time in producing another litter. With these cubs I was able to keep in touch until they were seventeen-and-a-half months old and ready to fend for themselves. By that time Pippa had already severed her links with them and had started a third litter, which she lost to a hyena when the cubs were thirteen days old. As to the fourth litter, we could almost say we had brought them up together till they were fourteen months old. Then Pippa broke a shoulder in a fight. The vets did their utmost to save her and I stayed with her in the Nairobi animal hospital for eighteen days – alas she died of heart failure. We buried her at our camp. We tried immediately to find the cubs but it took us a month. Luckily, when we saw them they proved to be in excellent condition, having obviously managed to kill enough game to keep going, though they gladly accepted food from us for the next three months. By then they had reached puberty and showed great interest in the opposite sex. With my camera, I was able to record their love-play which till then no one had witnessed in the wild. In 1971, to my great regret, I was obliged to leave the Meru Park as my agreement with the Park authorities for cheetah research had terminated. I have written Pippa's story in two books: *The Spotted Sphinx* and *Pippa's Challenge*. In these I describe the habits of cheetahs, discuss the reasons for their decline under natural conditions and why they breed with such difficulty in zoos. I also tell of my interest in the way in which cheetahs, and lions too, can control their breeding. Though they go into oestrus every few weeks, they will not let a male come near them while they are rearing a litter, which is a full-time job, for seventeen-and-a-half months with cheetahs and twenty months with lions.

On the other hand, after Pippa had lost her first and third litters, she went instantly to find a mate and immediately became pregnant. Another point of interest was that when Pippa wanted a mate, she did not appear to look around for one, she made a bee-line over eight miles to the nearest male, with whom she then remained for a week and conceived.

Observing Elsa's and Pippa's families made me aware that these animals appear to be able to communicate with each other over long distances and also, sometimes, seem to be aware of our intentions even when we are far away. There are of course rare cases of telepathy amongst human beings and this makes me wonder whether having developed our capacity to speak and write has not caused a sense which we once shared with animals to atrophy.

Meanwhile, George, who had resigned from the Game Department in 1961, decided to rehabilitate Boy, Girl and Ugas, three of the lions who had played in the film of *Born Free*. His base was twelve miles from mine. We could not camp nearer to each other because of the enmity between lions and cheetahs.

Having successfully rehabilitated Elsa and Pippa, and having seen their breeding habits, I now wanted to repeat the experiment with leopards, which are reputed to be the most dangerous and most intelligent of all African animals. Being nocturnal and elusive they would be difficult to study but I could not resist the challenge. So, when the Director of the National Parks offered me two leopard cubs I was thrilled, and started off for Nairobi to collect them. It proved fortunate that George's assistant, Tony Baxendale, followed an hour behind me. Going up a slope, with a steep drop on one side to a river, I came round a bend to see two Africans holding hands as they walked along the middle of the road. I hooted but they paid no attention. Finally, I was obliged to pass them. At that point the murram was loose, I skidded, hit a milestone and the Land-Rover rolled down the escarpment.

When I came round I found myself lying on splinters of glass, the Land-Rover was half-way down the hill and the African who had been travelling with me was sitting close by, holding his head. Judging by the position of the Land-Rover, it must have somersaulted down the escarpment. Fortunately, it had been caught on some bushes before it reached the river at the bottom. To my great relief the African had only a slight cut on his head. I was badly bruised and when I looked at my right hand, I saw that it was just a pulp of blood, flesh and earth.

I could hardly bear the pain as I struggled up the hill back to the road. There I collapsed. After some time, a lorry filled with Africans approached and stopped. Among the passengers was a local chief; he poured iodine on to my hand and as I felt no pain I realised that the injury must be a very severe one. The chief then helped me on to his lorry but before we started off for the nearest dispensary Tony Baxendale caught up with us. He helped me into his Land-Rover and asked the chief to guard the wreckage until the police came to investigate the accident.

We then drove eighty miles to the nearest hospital which was at Embu. The road was bumpy and I suffered a lot of pain and lost much blood. At the hospital my wounds were dressed and disinfected and I was given a pain-killer, after which we drove to Nairobi Hospital.

We did not get there till midnight; nevertheless, my friend, the surgeon Gerald Nevill, operated immediately but for the moment he could only graft skin from my leg on to the back of my hand. I was told that I would have to wait six months before the severed tendons and broken bones could be dealt with. I am totally right-handed and it was terrible for me to lose the use of my most important tool and with it, to some extent, my independence. It did not take me long to realise that unless my hand could be put right I would never again be able to play the piano, nor paint in the detailed manner which I like. I was also, of course, very disappointed to have to give up the leopard project, at any rate for the moment. While still in hospital I learned to type with my left hand.

Six months later I flew to London for a major operation which I hoped might give me back the use of my hand, but though five more operations followed over the next few years, I finally had to accept the fact that I was only going to be able to use my thumb and, to a limited extent, my index finger. During one of those operations, in 1969, I was told by a nurse of an exhibition of my tribal paintings running now in London. As soon as I was mobile I went there incognito and found the place crowded with visitors, apparently very interested in the originals, as well as in many life-size reproductions. I then learned from the organiser of this show that he had obtained permission from the trustees of the Nairobi Museum, who were by now the owners of my collection, to reproduce fifty-six of my portraits and to sell them all over the world for their mutual benefit. I was stunned. It had taken more than six years to paint about 700 pictures and I had barely been financially compensated for the expenses involved. Now, if I wanted to include a few of my paintings in a book, I had to pay royalties to the trustees – and like other customers I had to purchase any of the prints shown here. The only satisfaction I derived from all this was knowing that my paintings seemed to be popular. I had a proof of this when I was invited by the Governor, Malcolm MacDonald, to have tea with him and Jomo Kenyatta a few days before Independence. I could hardly believe my eyes when I saw my tribal paintings hanging on the walls. They had been beautifully mounted and framed. The Governor, who had always been interested in my pictorial records and had given me valuable advice when I was writing *The Peoples of Kenya*, had stressed the importance of this collection to Kenyatta. Together they had selected 300 of the best pictures for Government House – now to be named the State House. When I expressed surprise at seeing portraits of the Somali-Shifta who were giving much trouble at the time, hanging next to respected chiefs, Jomo Kenyatta said, smiling, 'Good or bad, they are all equally important to the history of Kenya.'

For years I had been looking for a house where George and I could live when we were both too old for bush life. Eventually I found a place that seemed to combine all we wished for. The property was in the Rift Valley, on Lake Naivasha and within an hour's drive of the Lake Nakuru National Park, while to the north lay the Aberdare National Park which rises to 9,000 feet above the small township of that name.

In the lichen-covered forest which grows on part of this mountain range lives the evasive bongo, while buffaloes and antelopes graze on its tussocked moorlands. Waterfalls bordered by delphiniums, red-hot pokers and cushions of everlastings, thunder down thousands of feet into narrow valleys.

It would be impossible to imagine a more attractive site for a home and I thought myself very lucky to be able to buy fifty acres right on the water-front. The estate even comprised a small indigenous forest of *Acacia xanthophloea*, commonly known as 'fever tree'. This name originated in the early days of Kenya when these beautiful, yellow-barked trees were associated with malaria-infested areas. Luckily there is no malaria around this lake which is at an altitude of 6,200 feet and has an ideal climate.

We decided to call our home Elsamere. Kenya is sometimes described as a cold country with a hot sun; this is particularly true of Naivasha where I often wear a cardigan on the open verandah, but change into a bathing suit before I move on to the lawn.

The area is becoming one of the most popular places for people living in Nairobi to go bird-watching, fishing or water-skiing but luckily our land is hidden from our neighbours, and from the road which connects the farms that are sited around the fifty-square-mile lake.

The property is at the end of an obsidian lava-flow emanating from the volcanic hinterland, which forms a ridge and projects at a steep slope into the lake; this prevents the house from ever being flooded during the frequent rises in the level of the lake. Another asset is the deep water along our promontory, which ensures that our bank is free from the wide papyrus belt which grows almost everywhere along the lake-front. The absence of papyrus enables us to fish from the land for *Tilapia nilotica* and black bass, both of which have been introduced into the lake and make very good eating.

The neighbouring papyrus belt is the home of countless birds and also shelters many hippos who spend the day there emerging only after dark to feed on the land. They made a habit of ambling on to our lawn which soon looked like a battlefield, and when they came near the house kept us awake with their rhythmic munchings and deep boomings. Sometimes I tried to drive them away by yelling or shining the beam of a powerful flashlight into their eyes. But they soon got used to my harmless eccentricities and went on munching. As they had all the forest in which to graze I felt justified in driving them off our land. I enquired about the best way to do this and was told to block their path with long logs placed over a foot high from the ground, for hippos cannot bend their legs more than a foot, so would be unable to clamber over them. We, therefore, placed logs all along the lake-front and sure enough these kept the hippos away.

The area close to the lake is ideal farming land because of its fertile volcanic soil, perfect climate and unlimited irrigation. This combination yields superb crops except on our property where, due to the obsidian flow, the surface soil is very shallow.

It was not long before I discovered that the ground here was literally strewn with prehistoric tools chipped out of obsidian. I have always been interested in archaeology and so I was thrilled when I learned that our new home was on a site where prehistoric man had once lived.

Our lake lies in the chain of the Rift Valley Lakes which are all brackish except for Baringo and Naivasha, which are fed by rivers. Originally all these lakes formed a vast sea; when it gradually receded, it left traces of the various water levels in the form of crustacean deposits, now mined under the name of diotermite.

Close to Elsamere is the famous 'Hell's Gate', a nine-mile-long gorge which it is thought may have been the outflow of this prehistoric sea. Now, its impressive cliffs are the home of many interesting birds, including the rare lammergeier which ornithologists from all over the world come to observe.

Some twenty years ago Lake Naivasha was surrounded by a large natural forest. The great curtain of dense undergrowth made up of creepers covering deadwood or hanging in profusion from the trees, at certain seasons, attracts myriads of lake flies. These are a nuisance near houses so the undergrowth had been cut down along the lake, with the result that the lake flies have been reduced to the minimum, but so have all the wild animals that depend on the forest belt for food and shelter. We have preserved our own little forest patch and it has become one of the last refuges for wild creatures. All around they are being trapped or shot or, as they come from the waterless hinterland to the lake for a drink, run over by traffic. When they found that at Elsamere they were not only safe from traps but had a secure access to the lake, as well as food and shelter in the forest, they began to appear in large numbers.

At first, I caught glimpses of antelopes and occasionally heard the coarse bark of a bushbuck at night; but soon these shy creatures came into the open and I was able to watch them in the early mornings nibbling grass, and while breakfasting a reedbuck often keeps me company.

Now that I have lived at Elsamere for several years, I have made friends with all the smaller creatures; the otters, a serval cat, a waterbuck, a civet, a genet, a spring hare, a long-tailed mongoose, a marsh mongoose, a ratel, a reedbuck, a bushbuck, duikers and dik-diks. The larger animals such as zebras, lions, eland, buffaloes and giraffes keep to the hills and only venture out after dark to go to the lake to drink.

When we bought the place there was a small stone house on it; we added a few rooms, knocked down some walls, exchanged the tiny windows for large ones and increased our view of the lake by means of large glass sliding doors. Having lived in the N.F.D. I was used to open spaces and I preferred a few big rooms to a lot of small ones. We brought our furniture from Isiolo. It had been made by an Italian prisoner of war, is simple and of excellent design. Since over the years we have collected artifacts from all round the world, our rooms have a cosmopolitan character.

I have, of course, kept my piano (which I played so long as I could use both my hands) and our books fill the bookcases which stand in every space not occupied by large windows or sliding glass doors.

My taste for large rooms has proved very useful as I am frequently visited by tourist groups of twenty to thirty people and there is space for them to mingle comfortably.

Perhaps the most important 'room' is the outdoor wired-in enclosure which I built for a leopard cub I hoped to rehabilitate. Unfortunately, this cub died but the enclosure became very useful when later on I nursed various sick animals.

George has his quarters consisting of a bedroom, dressing-room, bathroom, small office and an open verandah at one end of the house. I have my bedroom-cum-working room and bathroom at the other end, though mostly I use the open verandah as my 'office' during the day and work indoors after dark. The space between George's suite and mine and the guest rooms is connected by a large sitting-dining room opening on to an equally large verandah which can be closed in a minute by sliding glass doors. This is what we do when we sit there for a sun-downer and watch the animals outside.

Beyond the house is an annexe with a garage and three rooms; one is a guest room, one is used for tents, luggage and safari kit and the third is a workroom for George, who likes to do carpentry and mechanical repairs.

When George brought his lion, Boy, who had been dangerously ill, to our home in order that he could be treated for eight months by our vet, he built himself a bungalow at some distance from the house. In this way he could be always at hand by night and by day to look after Boy and give him moral support.

When the patient recovered George took him to his camp on the Tana River. This was a journey of 400 miles and one which has to be made in four-wheel-drive cars. As a result we are not able to see each other as often as we would wish.

Even though I had intended to live at Elsamere only after George and I were too old for a more active life in the bush, it now became my home over the years when I needed medical treatment for my injured right hand. During this time I could not commit myself to an uninterrupted period of up to several years in which to study leopards. I did, however, travel for short periods between my operations. This was necessary to develop the various Elsa Wild Animal Appeals, which by now are established internationally.

Ever since I had launched the Elsa Appeal in England, I had

Exhibition of Joy's tribal paintings
at the Indian Tea Centre, London

Addressing a press conference in Budapest, 1971.
Minister Földes sitting, interpreter standing next to Joy

A friendly dolphin

An irresistible
koala bear at Perth,
Australia

Making a graft
on the Friendship Tree
at Sochi, Black Sea

Joy offers a maize cob to a Przevalsky horse
at Askaniya Nova, Ukraine

Entertaining visitors from the USA at Elsamere

realised what an important part Elsa held in the increasing world-wide movement for preserving wildlife, especially in the U.S.A. Encouraged by donations I received from schoolchildren who collected funds for Elsa by organising raffles, cake sales and other money-raising efforts, I persuaded the Trustees of the Elsa Appeal in London to launch a similar appeal in the U.S.A., as I believed that the book royalties which financed the appeal in England could not guarantee for ever the necessary funds, but that our work could be carried on in the States. We set up a Board of Trustees in California for the purpose of establishing the Elsa Wild Animal Appeal as a non-profit-making organisation. This took the best part of four years to organise.

Meanwhile, the schoolchildren collected funds in Elsa's name and started the first official Elsa Club in Missouri. Other schools followed and now, in 1978, the Elsa Clubs number over 400 and operate throughout the U.S.A.

To facilitate educational information available to the clubs, a beautifully illustrated teaching kit is published every year, which is the result of intense research on the habits of wild animals and how to prevent their extermination.

Stimulated by the success of the Elsa Wild Animal Appeal in the U.S.A., Canada founded the E.W.A.A. in 1971.

In 1975 I was invited to establish the appeal in Japan under the name of Elsa's Nature Conservancy.

Although each organisation works independently according to the laws of the country, all involved pursue the same policy with emphasis on educating people in the value of wildlife conservation. All work for the establishment of National Parks and Game Reserves and do research on the habits of wild animals living under natural conditions.

Apart from the E.W.A.A. now operating in England, the U.S.A., Canada, Kenya and Japan, we use the book royalties earned in Russia, Poland, Hungary, Czechoslovakia, Roumania and Bulgaria to help wild animals in those countries and I am glad to know from annual reports that Elsa is not only popular but also beneficial to the wildlife behind the Iron Curtain.

13

Pippa's Grandchildren

After I had to leave Meru I was very concerned about Pippa's descendants and realised that I could only learn of their development and breeding by periodic visits to Meru.

During the first four trips I was lucky to find two of the second litter, Tatu with two cubs of her own and Whity with one male cub.

Whity had been seen several times by visitors together with a cub who was extremely shy. When I found them one morning near a swamp, both were resting under a bush. As soon as I approached them in a Land-Rover the cub bolted, though Whity let me drive to within a few yards without moving. Local, the African ranger who had helped me during the years I had camped in the Meru, remained with me inside the car. We were silent, hoping the cub would return. He did so after Whity called to him in a soft moan which seemed to reassure him that we could be trusted. Both cheetahs spent the midday heat dozing under a bush until it was cool enough for them to become active. To test Whity's memory, I offered her water in the old tin she had always drunk from as a cub. She came along for a drink, apparently as relaxed as if we had not been parted for three and a half years.

At first the cub ran away but when I got into the car, he came back and tried to taste the liquid in this strange container. At this Whity nipped him, preventing him from getting near the tin and finally chased him away. She then continued lapping and even when I came within touching distance of her to add Ideal milk to the water, she showed not the slightest nervousness. When she had had her fill, she moved off slowly.

To my astonishment her cub now reappeared and cautiously approached the tin. Sniffing at the diluted milk, he wrinkled his nose in disgust and ran quickly after his mother. Both then ambled out of view. Whity still treated me as a friend and had even transferred her trust in me to her cub.

On my next safari to Meru in May 1972 I was again accompanied by good old Local, who had been an integral part of my past life in Meru, and we were both happy that he could carry on during my return.

Now as we passed a tree Local grabbed me by my shoulder and whispered, 'Look at what you have nearly stepped on.' Within a few inches of my feet was the coil of a large python immobilised by a huge object inside her. The snake must have just swallowed a buck the size of a Grant's gazelle; as a result she was incapable of defending herself and even a small jackal could have bitten her head off. Local told me that it might take a month or more before the python had finished digesting her enormous meal. How little she could move we realised when very slowly she slithered under a nearby bush, which certainly would not protect her from predators but made her less conspicuous than she had been in the open. I was impressed by the way in which a python's skin could expand in order to stretch over a kill – each scale was separated from the next one by as much as an inch.

During the next few days we made a point of visiting the snake. It was still under the same bush and well hidden except for the white lumps of calcium excrement.

We often followed vultures circling above a spot, hoping that they might lead us to a kill made by Pippa's cubs, but they only guided us to lion kills. However interesting these were, they added to my anxiety because lions and cheetahs do not get on. On two occasions when we were investigating thorn bushes, expecting to find our cheetahs under their shade, we saw lions sneaking away. Obviously we had interfered with their midday siesta but luckily they were too sleepy to attack us; or perhaps they may have realised that we meant them no harm.

Our days were full of interesting incidents and some of our nights in camp were equally exciting.

Often I heard faint whuffs as the lions came to investigate the tents, then I felt as if I were back in the past, for how often had I been conscious of lions close to camp, while knowing that they would never betray their presence.

This visit to Meru coincided with the annual migration of the elephants and since the camp was sited on their usual route we saw plenty of them. One evening as I was sitting right in the open in my little canvas bath, enjoying the warm air and looking at the stars, two elephants emerged as silently as ghosts out of the dark and moved swiftly towards me. I rushed into the tent, more for moral support than for protection, and luckily the giants went on to look for a drinking place higher up the stream.

Another time I was woken up by rhythmic munching close to the tent. Assuming that it came from a feeding buffalo, I looked through the small window of the tent and faced the huge bulk of an elephant so close that it blacked out everything else. There was no time to contact Local so I could do nothing but yell. This made the giant turn, after a few paces he looked back, seemingly puzzled by the strange noise. At this I yelled again, he swerved round and eventually faded into the darkness.

If a day in the bush is never dull, there are, however, often frustrating periods. It was on one such trying day that, as we staggered across a lava plateau, we observed a few isolated acacia bushes. They were of the type our cheetahs had always preferred to lie under during the hot hours, using the shady cover as a spot from which they could watch everything that was happening on the plain without being seen.

Local had gone to investigate some bushes further off and I was thinking how fruitless the last ten days had been, for we had not even found spoor on the hard ground. Suddenly there was a rustle and out of the acacia shot Whity and her three cubs. I recognised her instantly, not only by the markings at the root of her tail, but also by her face as she stopped and looked at me before trotting off calling to her bolting offspring. I followed until she stopped on an outcrop from which she could survey the plain. She let me come within ten yards of her while the cubs hid behind her. Whity seemed completely relaxed, until suddenly her eyes narrowed and she spotted Local in the far distance. Then she ran away with her family, making for a little stream which she crossed. I rushed after her and was just in time to see one of the cubs splash into the shallow water and disappear with Whity into some bushes at the far side. I sat still, waiting for Local to catch up, and hoping to see the other cubs; after twenty minutes we both crossed the water and searched for the family. We found them under a tree. One cub stayed close to his mother while another moved around nervously some five yards away. Whity then gave the very low cheetah moan which I knew so well from occasions when Pippa uttered the call if worried about a cub. Now, a faint chirp resembling a bird call came from the third cub. While looking at me without any sign of fear Whity began to lick one of the cubs that was cuddling up to her. Not to alarm the family I remained some twenty yards away while Local kept at a much greater distance.

When I had been in Meru ten months earlier I had seen Whity with her male cub, who was almost old enough to hunt on his own. She must have abandoned him soon afterwards and started this present litter. With a gestation of ninety-three days, I reckoned that the new cubs were about four months old. I felt very happy; it was wonderful that Whity had reared three cubs up to this age in an area frequented by lions. Local, however, was sure that there were four cubs in the litter and proved to be right.

Now it was time to go home if we wanted to reach camp before dark. Early next morning we returned and I spotted the family close to where we had left them. They ran away and it took us most of the day to trace their spoor. In the late afternoon we passed a bush, from which Whity and four cubs suddenly emerged, leaving the remains of a young bushbuck carcass behind. Following at a distance of some thirty yards, I observed the cubs. Two of them were larger and of a lighter colour than the others; I assumed these might be males. Unfortunately, a cloudburst made it impossible to photograph them.

Next day we found the family at the same place. Later Whity took the cubs into a valley bounded by two little streams. She moved to the one furthest away from us, where I had seen fresh lion spoor a few days ago and also noticed a troop of baboons. Intending to prevent her from going there, I quickly moved in a large circle between the cheetah and the stream. Whity seemed puzzled by my manoeuvre and advanced to within eight yards of me before stopping and growling. Obviously she did not mind my being around but she wasn't going to put up with my interfering with her plans. I stood my ground until she turned back. The cubs had kept at a safe distance and were now well ahead of us. After a short time Whity turned towards me, persisting in her intention of crossing the stream again. I cut her off by moving slowly towards her until she gave up and settled with her cubs under a tree. I sat within fifteen yards of her and tried to photograph the family, but the clicking of the shutter made the cubs very jittery so I put the Leica away. One of the smaller cubs was particularly nervous and bolted at my slightest movement, chirping for help; a larger cub went to console her until Whity came to her rescue and brought her back. All the cubs were in excellent condition and Whity appeared to be the most protective mother. Sitting there and watching her family dozing off I was moved to see our Whity, whom we had rescued in the nick of time when she broke her leg, who had had to be confined in my camp for several weeks and had hated every moment of it, but who now after five and a half years, treated me as a friend and trusted me, even to the point of sharing her cubs with me.

At midday the family fell asleep. Assuming that they would not move during the hot hours, I left them as my time in Meru was running short and I wanted to search for Tiny, Big Boy and Somba, the cubs of Pippa's fourth litter.

Next day we came across a pride of eight lions on a waterbuck kill within less than half a mile of where Whity had been and twenty-four hours later we surprised three lions in the same area, fast asleep; they were obviously annoyed at being disturbed and they now reluctantly sneaked away. The presence of all these lions explained why Whity had left, but how could she know that they were coming the day before they arrived?

Although we could not find our cheetahs again during the rest of my stay in the Meru, it was wonderful to see the countryside so green and every bush bursting into bloom – a sure sign of the coming rains. I had always wondered why blossom appeared two to three weeks before the breaking of the rains; in time I learned it is one of nature's wise precautions to ensure pollination. During this period the atmosphere is already humid enough to encourage flowering and so pollination can be completed before the heavy rains batter the blossoms to the ground.

Just before I left we found the family's spoor going from the lava plateau, down a ridge, to a plain some four miles from where we had last seen the cheetahs. It seemed to be two days old. By then it was too dark to follow it up so, as I had to leave next morning, I decided to break camp at dawn and search as best as we could on our way out.

After tracking across very difficult ground, I spotted a tree heavily loaded with vultures. Approaching it cautiously, in case there might be lions on the kill, I saw our cubs tucking in at the unopened carcass of a young Grant's gazelle, while Whity, still panting from the effort of the hunt, rested close by.

Though I crept very slowly towards them, the cubs ran away, but when Whity called 'Prr, prr' they stopped and then returned. One of the smaller cubs seemed especially frightened. As soon as they had settled on the kill I tried to take photographs, but again the clicking (even at a distance of about thirty yards) caused the cubs to bolt to a termite hill some 200 yards away. Whity did her best to call them back, but they did not budge until I moved away and only when I was at a safe distance did they rush to the kill, which by now Whity had opened for them. For half an hour I watched them through my field glasses, gorging themselves on the gazelle. Whity stood by but gave them priority. When just the head and feet remained, the vultures ventured to land, then it was fun to see the cubs dashing into the feathered crowd to send them flying. Even though only four to five months old, the little cheetahs were evidently already used to defending their kill.

I recalled similar scenes, remembering what a good mother Pippa had been to each of her families while they were still dependent on her. In contrast, once the cubs were able to fend for themselves, she cut her ties with them so that on the few occasions when they met, she greeted them with a growl and chased them away.

Considering that the ties with their mother had been much stronger than their relationship with me, it seemed incredible that Pippa's cubs (Tatu and Whity) retained their trust in me, although we had parted five and a half years ago. Not only were they willing to share their cubs with me, but would do so even when on a kill – a time when no predator will tolerate intruders.

Of course I was most anxious to know how Whity would succeed in rearing her cubs. So three months later I went back to Meru. Again I camped with Local at Pippa's former home. In the evening I sat by her grave. All was very still except for the wind tossing through the two large tamarind trees which over-shadow the place; it got stronger during the night and often changed direction. Perhaps this accounted for the presence of the many hornbills – in the early morning I counted 130 flying from the stream to the plains. When I lived here with Pippa, I knew of two pairs residing near the camp but never had I seen such a number before.

As usual when we arrive at the camp after an absence, the wild animals, who by night use the site as a drinking place, have to get used to our presence. So I was not surprised when on the first night a rhino snorted close to my tent, but luckily trotted off before I had even shone the torch on him. The second night four lions walked quietly round the car, went to the kitchen and passed within a few yards of me. I had barricaded the entrance to my tent, which I had left open because of the heat, with a table and a chair. I knew that as a rule animals are simply inquisitive and will do no harm unless provoked. Next morning we saw a lioness with a small cub not far from camp, resting under a tree. She showed no sign of nervousness when we passed in the car within ten yards of her. In the course of the third night I heard the sound of lapping, an identifiable lion-lap. Later my tent shook as a lion cub stumbled against a rope and jumped off with a growl. Switching on my torch, I observed six lions between the tent and the kitchen. They were evidently quite relaxed since they were licking themselves and uttering low grunts. Though I told them to go away, they stayed on for some time.

During these days we found several spoor of single cheetah, amongst them one which I assumed to be that of Pippa's mate because it was near all the landmarks he used to visit.

Since I left Meru in January 1970, Local's job had been to look after three pairs of white rhinos which had been imported from South Africa in the hope that they would breed here. He was proud of his charges, who now roamed freely through the park, and liked to show how he could control them. On the few occasions when we met them in the bush, he walked up to them, patted them and talked to them.

One morning we spotted a rhino grazing near a rivulet. He was so absorbed with his meal that he did not get our wind until we were within a few yards of him. As he lifted his head, I realised that this was not one of the tame white rhino but a very wild black rhino. He charged instantly, leaping across the stream. Local and I ran for our lives only to come face to face with two elephants. Luckily they turned off our path and we were able to sneak between them and the rhino to reach safer ground.

Day after day we searched in vain all the places that were good cheetah country and had been frequented by Pippa's families.

One afternoon when we were walking beside the Rojoweru river I heard a splash and saw a monster crocodile at least fifteen feet in length, submerging. Another splash followed as a lion jumped to the far bank where he disappeared. Cautiously peeping through the river-bush, I almost stepped on a lioness who then plunged into the river to join her mate. All three had been feasting on the carcass of a buffalo, which must have been killed by the lions. What surprised me was that the lions had tolerated a crocodile sharing their kill with them. Perhaps this crocodile was too large for them to chase off without provoking an attack.

When, after two more days of futile search for Whity, we again passed the spot, I was even more surprised to see eight monster crocodiles, each of them fourteen to fifteen feet long, crawling into the stomach cavity of the carcass and pushing each other aside in their greed. A gruesome feature of the scene was that, while having their macabre meal, their snouts made them look as if they were laughing.

Another day we followed vultures and found a dead elephant.

It had been killed three or four days earlier. The trunk, tusks, ears and tail had been removed by the poachers, now the vultures were finishing off what carrion was left. Poaching outside the border of this park was very heavy, but to find one of the victims right inside was most alarming. It made me worry about Pippa's offspring, as the value of a cheetah pelt is well known to poachers.

I then remembered that recently we had come across a baobab tree with a hollow trunk which had evidently been used by poachers as a hideout and store, for pegs rammed inside the cavity walls suggested that this was where they had hung up their loot.

One evening as I sat by Pippa's grave, I felt sure I was being watched. I stared into the darkness but could not see anything so I rose to get a better view; at this moment a lion's head popped up some twenty yards away. He looked at me for a few seconds and then sank back into the grass. I wondered if lions used the large cairn on Pippa's grave as a convenient look-out to watch animals coming to drink at the rivulet.

On another occasion we crossed a long causeway which formed the top of a weir over the Rojoweru river. Waddling through the shallow water were a pair of Egyptian geese with seven tiny goslings, the little ones barely, as yet, able to walk. Suddenly, to my horror I noticed the tip of a crocodile's nose not far away, just visible above the water – obviously the croc was waiting for a snack. Hoping to save the goslings I blew the horn; at this the crocodile somersaulted over the weir into the river below, while the parent geese ushered their flock as fast as they could across the causeway into the river-bush. At least, for the moment, the family was safe but I wondered how many of the seven goslings would live to reach maturity.

Walking in the hills we came across a crescent-shaped bluff overgrown with raffia palms; at its base were several crystal-clear pools filled by springs rising on higher ground. It was an idyllic spot. The many spoor and droppings of various animals gave ample proof of what went on here by night and now even in daylight we saw, hardly visible under overhanging palm fronds, two elephants standing in a pool.

While having lunch not far away, we watched several reticulated giraffe coming towards us. Although they are smaller than their *Masaica* cousins who live in the higher parts of Kenya, with their clearly defined, net-like markings they are very attractive, indeed amongst the most beautiful animals of Africa. Two of the males seemed very interested in a female, who stood not far off. I watched the rivals walking slowly in circles round each other, banging their heads and touching each other's muzzles; it was all so gentle that until I saw their genitals I believed it was play. For about half an hour they continued this contest until the smaller bull moved off. The victor now approached the female, investigated her rectum, at which moment she urinated. The male licked the liquid and then followed the female. Finally they walked closely together into the bush. It had been the gentlest dispute for priority I had ever witnessed.

Less gentle were a group of seventeen elephants who, on seeing us, formed themselves into a phalanx in the centre of which were two very small calves. The adults flapped their ears and seemed ready to charge should we dare to come one step nearer.

At this moment I observed a paradise flycatcher trailing its delicate long tail through the thorny scrub, and was fascinated by the contrast between this frail form of life moving next to the most robust of all creatures.

By now I had searched unsuccessfully for twenty days for Whity and Tatu, my time was running out and I was getting desperate. Then, unexpectedly we met two visitors who told us that they had just seen a cheetah with four cubs at a bush near the road. We drove there. The cheetah had gone, but we saw fresh spoor and after following it for two hot hours I spotted Whity and her cubs under a tree. Hoping that we could get nearer by car, I collected the Land-Rover, but as soon as I turned it off the road, the cubs bolted. I waited until the family settled again and, leaving Local in the car, walked slowly to within fifty yards of them and sat down. I was happy to see that all four cubs were still alive, they must have been eight months old by now. How Whity had succeeded in protecting them against so many lions and other predators, I could not imagine. The smallest of the cubs was still very nervous and kept in hiding most of the time. Obviously it knew its physical handicap and took no chances.

I showed Whity the familiar tin to which she quickly reacted, lapping up the water within two yards of me. The cubs ran away, but when Whity reassured them with her 'Prr, prr' they returned for their midday siesta, after which I took pictures of them, as they were too sleepy to protest. At 5 p.m. they started yawning and stretching and then moved away slowly. The nervous cub went ahead and Whity walked in the direction from which I heard it calling.

It was a beautiful sight to watch them ambling along in the tall grass, which shone like gold against the setting sun and contrasted brilliantly with the deep-red rain curtain that overhung the indigo-coloured hills along the horizon.

I felt that even if I should never see Whity again, she had achieved all I had wished for her: to live free in this beautiful park, giving birth to litter after litter which in turn would produce their own families. Whity was the link between Pippa and these wild cubs. My experiment had proved that these cats can be saved from extermination by breeding them under natural conditions.

In January 1976 I took some friends to Meru for two days. I never expected to see Pippa's offspring during such a short stay, though I became excited by the report that recently a cheetah with three small cubs had been seen near the Rojoweru river. Since this flows partly through Whity's territory, I hoped that it might be her. Early and late we concentrated our searches within this area, knowing that during the heat of the day the cheetah would be well hidden. During this time we drove through other parts of the park, where we saw almost every animal which lived in Meru except for leopards and cheetahs. The elephants had so many tiny calves that we got quite annoyed when we saw a herd without any youngsters. The same was true of giraffes, among whom we found baby-sitters – one female watching several young while their mothers went browsing.

On our last evening we crept once more along the road running parallel to the Rojoweru and suddenly I noticed a cheetah's head emerging from the grass not more than ten yards away.

When I called quietly 'Whity' she ignored the sound, but did not bolt as any wild cheetah would have done. Thus encouraged

I poured water into the familiar tin, stepped slowly out of the car, and walked cautiously forward. The cheetah turned and I was able to identify Whity by the spots along the root of her tail. I was half-way to her, she made no attempt to come to the water bowl but gazed ahead. Following the direction of her eyes, I saw four Grant's gazelles in the far distance. As she was obviously more interested in prey than in the water, I got back into the car from where we watched her. She moved steadily towards the gazelles, stalking them step by step, being very careful to freeze if they raised their heads and looked at her.

This went on for half an hour after which Whity sank into the high grass and disappeared from view. There was no cover between her and the gazelles and the distance was evidently too great for her to risk a final rush.

We waited for another half-hour, by which time the Grant's gazelles had moved off. Whity now emerged and uttered a very faint low moan, a sound which indicated that she was calling her cubs, while taking care not to attract predators.

At once there was movement in the grass and we saw three white tail-tips. They belonged to three cubs about three months old. Rushing towards Whity, they jumped on her, falling over each other in their efforts to get close. Whity did not stop to lick them, but moved on with her little ones gambolling beside her. The light was fading rapidly and we caught a few glimpses of the youngsters rolling down a little termite hill before their mother took them out of our view and disappeared into the dark plain.

We returned early next morning to see if Whity had made a kill. Not far from where we had left the family we saw vultures dispersing in a spiral flight, but we could not find a trace of a kill or of the cheetahs.

Now I could only pray that Whity would succeed in rearing this new litter as successfully as she had reared her previous families. I knew that she had been pregnant six times but what happened to two of her litters I never discovered; she was now nine years and five months old, and had lived completely wild for seven years and ten months.

14

Some of
My Neighbours

It was in June 1970 that George and I first began to observe a pair of Colobus monkeys that were living at Elsamere.

As they leapt from tree to tree with outstretched arms, their long black and white hair flowing like a cape behind them, they looked more like fairy creatures than monkeys. Colobus live in groups, each dominated by a male. They utter deep roars that can be heard for over a mile and which may last up to twenty minutes.

One day while we were watching our pair high up in a tree, the branch on which the female was sitting broke; she fell 100 feet and landed with a thud. I feared that she might have injured herself, but to my relief she picked herself up and disappeared with her mate.

I did not see them again for sixteen days; when I did they were deep in the forest, the female sitting hunched up and still. I noticed something purple that I thought was one of her hands, so I imagined she had damaged it in her fall. Then I took out my field glasses and discovered that what I had taken for a hand was in fact the face of a baby, and that a white tail, about five inches long, was dangling over the mother's arm. The little monkey was white all over except for its pale purple face. Ten days later it developed black ears to match its large black eyes. I named it Coli.

Not long afterwards I had to go away for a month; when I

returned, Coli's hands and feet had become black, his arms and face were grey and his forehead was divided from the rest of his face by a thin white line. Mother and child were devoted to each other. The father usually remained at a distance from them but kept a sharp look-out for any possible danger.

I had always believed that a monkey's ability to jump from branch to branch was innate but now, when I saw Coli hopping from one parent's shoulder to the other, I realised that day by day they widened the distance he would have to cover and so developed his sense of balance.

He soon became a very busy little monkey, dangling by one arm from a branch, twiddling round and round, and swinging to and fro. He had also become very cheeky, sometimes swinging a branch against one of his parents and even pulling leaves out of their mouths. For this he always got spanked.

When he found himself unable to climb a tree because the bark was too smooth and the trunk too wide, his mother would help him by placing herself on a fork above him and letting her tail hang down for him to use as a rope-ladder.

The family was now quite used to us and remained placidly on their trees when we were around, but if visitors came they made for the forest. When the rains began this was a new experience for Coli, but he seldom got wet as for most of the time his mother covered him with her arms, spreading her cape protectively around his body. It was interesting to see the way in which the family departed to the tops of the trees when a storm was heavy. I assumed they did this to avoid falling branches.

Again I had to leave Elsamere for some weeks; on my return I was greeted by the news that one of the parent monkeys had been missing for two weeks.

Early next morning we started to search and in the afternoon found the father dead in a tree. When we got the body down we saw that he had been riddled with shot-gun pellets. My neighbour was away at the time and had left his staff with a shot-gun and some dogs to defend the property; undoubtedly they had killed the Colobus, hoping to get a few shillings for his skin or sell his tail as a fly whisk.

At once I set out to find Coli and his mother and discovered them clinging to each other in some nearby trees. They remained there for two days and then moved nearer to the house.

Coli had grown considerably. I was also struck by how much older his mother's face had become and what deep furrows she had round her nose. It was sad to see her gazing into space while clasping little Coli who buried his head between her chin and knees. Their attitude expressed their sorrow. They were obviously very shocked and very unhappy and it was a long time before they began to play again.

In April 1972 I was rung up by a farmer who asked me if I would take a baby Colobus. Its mother had probably been killed by dogs when raiding vegetables. I hoped that at such an early age the baby would be adopted by my Colobus. I was delighted and drove over to fetch it. The farmer's daughter had looked after it and now I saw it peeping out from beneath her cardigan. Judging by its colour it must have been about two and a half months old.

When the girl handed it to me, it clung desperately to her woollen cardigan and only with great hesitation did it accept my blouse. It also refused to feed from the new bottle and I had to borrow the old one. I was told that the baby had taken very quickly to bottle feeding and that every two hours it drank Ideal milk diluted with two-thirds water mixed with a little glucose; a diet I had recommended over the telephone to the farmer. In its droppings there were remains of fibre, which indicated that it had already eaten leaves.

When we reached Elsamere it gave a little cry and, faint as this was, Coli and his mother came racing up to within a few feet of us and stared at the baby, evidently fascinated.

In the early morning Coli's mother called and the baby reacted instantly. I would have liked to let the little monkey join them but I thought it too great a risk, so I put it in the wire enclosure which George had originally built for his sick lion.

Later I was playing with the baby on the lawn when the telephone rang; I popped it into a crate and made for the house. When I returned the mother monkey was pushing her hand into the crate and the baby was clasping it. This made me decide to

George and Joy, 1976

Elsamere

Joy with Verreaux's eagle-owl

Baby Colobus playing at Elsamere

The Austrian Ambassador to Kenya, Dr. Ernst Illsinger,
presenting the 'Austrian Cross of Honour for Science
and Arts' to Joy Adamson in recognition of her contribution
to the conservation of wildlife. Nairobi, 1977.

let Coli and his mother take charge of the orphan.

I opened the door of the cage; in a flash the baby was out and hopping at top speed towards its adopted mother. Calling all the time, she met it on the ground, clutched it to her chest and raced up high into the tree with it. Instantly the baby stopped crying. As I watched the two through my field glasses hugging and cuddling each other, I wondered whether I had made the right decision. Would the mother be able to keep the baby alive though she had no milk? I also wondered whether the infant was old enough to nibble leaves, even though I had seen him put some into his mouth. My anxiety increased when after forty-eight hours I saw that the little fellow was getting thinner and thinner.

At dawn I heard the mother calling and found the baby hanging upside down in a thicket, only just alive. I carried him into the house, gave him some milk and glucose and kept him on my lap. We played together for some time till sadly his grip on my fingers relaxed and he ceased to breathe.

It was against this background that, in 1975, I rescued two one-year-old female Colobus who had been illegally purchased and kept in captivity for five months. I called them Long-tail and Short-tail; apart from this contrast in their physical appearance they had very different temperaments. Short-tail was quick and rather aggressive while Long-tail was slow and good-natured.

After two and a half months I felt I could safely let them go free in the forest to find their food. Both Coli and his mother had been much interested ever since their arrival though it took another five months before I saw the mother monkey with her arm round the shoulders of the two orphans who were cuddling up to her. They have now become an integrated and happy family.

If watching the Colobus monkeys has been a continuing pleasure to me, so has observing the Verreaux's eagle-owls, a pair of which lived in an abandoned fish eagle nest at the far end of our forest. These owls are the largest in Africa and their appearance is very striking for their black eyes, the size of ping-pong balls, are protected by bright pink eyelids fringed with white lashes, and their great hooked beak grows out of a fluffy moustache of feathers darker than those of their pale-grey face. Below the beak is a white beard. They have large horns lined with black feathers.

When I discovered an owlet half a mile away from the nest I was thrilled. The youngster could not as yet hoot but gave a whistling sound.

In German, *pfeifen* means to whistle and that is what I named the little owl. It certainly did a great deal of whistling when it was hungry.

In many species of owl the male is smaller than the female; judging by Pfeifer's size at so young an age I thought it obvious that she must be a female.

I was surprised to notice that very soon the father took over all the maternal duties and beak-fed his daughter while the mother sat aloof on a nearby tree.

When Pfeifer was five months old her horns developed and her colouring changed from grey to light-brown. She soon learned from her parents how to lie on the ground with widespread wings, and remain completely motionless. This might have been to sun herself or for 'anting', but more often I believe it was to trick the smaller birds into coming within her reach. They were certainly intrigued by an apparently dead owl and sometimes ventured fatally close.

Soon, whenever I called her she knew that I had food to give her and would sail in from the forest accompanied by her father who always had the first helping.

My feeding of the owls had gradually developed while we were clearing the ground around the house of mole-rats, which were most destructive for the lawn. The owls regarded these rodents as a great delicacy and gobbled two to three a day. But since those rats have a body length of some eight inches they occasionally got stuck when only half-way down the owls' throat, they then had to avoid choking by convulsive throw-ups. Concentrating on this painful operation, the owls closed their eyes and, with their bright pink eyelids and half a rat sticking from their beak, looked ludicrously pathetic.

One morning I found Pfeifer entangled in a vine. The more she struggled the more firmly she was caught. Eventually I went to her rescue and was surprised that she remained quite still as I freed her. Pfeifer was in every sense a wild owl and I had no intention of taming her, though gradually a bond developed between us and she seemed to trust me completely.

She showed this by walking in her typical sailor-gait slowly up to me shifting her weight from one white, fluffy-booted leg to the other whenever I held out meat, then taking it to the lawn and eating it within a few inches of me. I was often tempted to put my hands into her soft plumage, but I should never have forgiven myself if, by doing this, she became so tame that other human beings might become a danger to her.

About this time I was obliged to go away for a while. When I returned I found the mother bird incubating. Pfeifer now took on the task of feeding her mother. This was not always easy as her trips were observed by the fish eagles who often attacked her savagely. After another short absence I came back to find what looked like some white fluff just visible above the rim of the nest. It proved to be the head of a new chick.

In spite of continuing ambushes from the fish eagles and also from an augur buzzard, Pfeifer dutifully fed the latest arrival and indeed, she went on acting as nursery maid to the young owlet for a long time. I called it Bundu (which means owl in Kiswaheli). Like all young animals, the new arrival's eyes still had that soft, trusting expression which is so different from the hard glance of adult wild animals who are aware of the dangers surrounding them.

One day when Bundu was six months old she got entangled in some weed growing by the edge of the lake, and I found her hanging upside down, unable to move. When I had freed her I was surprised that she did not fly to the safety of the trees but hopped off even deeper into the undergrowth. Next morning I saw no sign of her but noticed Pfeifer staring at a spot near which I had last seen Bundu, and soon I discovered her in a pepper tree, very hungry. I fed and stroked her to see if she were injured. When I touched her right wing she flinched – assuming she was injured, I took her to the large outside enclosure where she would be safe from predators and I could watch her.

Pfeifer took up a position on a corner post of the enclosure, from where she watched her sister very closely. The owlet seemed so much better that I felt guilty at having locked her up. As Pfeifer was close by I decided to release her and see if she could fly across a greater distance than the enclosure allowed. Wrapping a towel over her I carried her outside.

It soon became apparent that Bundu was unable to fly. I asked a veterinary surgeon to come and examine her; Mr Cooper said she had a broken ulna and radius. After giving her an injection he told me that she should be confined for a month.

During this time I fed her and, since she seemed to need company, did my typing next to her and sometimes sketched her. Eventually when we released her she opened her wings and, after a perfect flight, landed on a tree some hundred yards away.

The monkeys who had been watching our activities now raced up to Bundu. Apparently they were happy to see that she had come back to their world. Pfeifer, too, was delighted and the sisters sat side by side, scratching each other's head.

Some weeks later Pfeifer went missing and it was a month before a local man saw her three miles away, near some fish eagles' nest. I went there and found her in the company of another owl. Soon afterwards she again vanished.

Many months later when I was feeding Bundu after dark, I saw Pfeifer fly in and behind her was a shy little owlet. I was happy that she trusted me to feed her chick and, indeed, I wondered if she were not telling the other owls, 'Let's take our chicks to eat at Elsamere, it will save us a lot of work.'

I named the new arrival Toto. It was a very plucky little owl. Soon it started to fly on to the lawn in search of food; occasionally there would be a swish as a fish eagle swooped down. Instantly Bundu, Pfeifer and the grandmother bird would come to the rescue and chase the intruder away.

There is a lot of wildlife at Elsamere but I think that the Colobus monkeys and the eagle-owls have given me more pleasure than any of the other creatures that live there.

15

Elsa's Legacy

The Elsa and the Pippa books made many people, the world over, aware of the disastrous plight of wild animals and of the efforts needed to save them from extinction.

As a result I was asked to visit several countries which, till then, I had few hopes of ever seeing.

Among some of my most memorable journeys were those to the U.S.S.R., Japan, Thailand and Hungary, where my press conference in Budapest was attended by Minister Földes.

Soon after my arrival in Moscow I was flown to Sochi, on the Black Sea, where I was asked to make a graft on the Friendship Tree. This citrus was planted in 1934; in 1940 the Soviet scientist Schmidt made the first graft which was of a species different to that of the citrus. It was followed by more grafts made by various distinguished people representing 126 different nationalities. Today the tree bears the fruit of Italian lemons, American grapefruit, oranges, pomelos, giant oyas and tiny kumquats. Some of the grafts were made in memory of celebrated people such as Charles Darwin and Louis Pasteur, and soil from the graves of Tolstoy, Tchaikovsky, Pushkin and Mahatma Gandhi has been placed at the foot of the tree. I was very happy to make a graft in Elsa's name to this tree of goodwill; it symbolises my hope that the work done in her name to save wildlife will become a movement drawing nations together in peace.

Not far from Sochi is the large Zapovednic Reserve. One of the chief aims of the directors is to breed the bison. The reserve contains fifty-nine species of mammals including 300 brown bears. It is one of 102 reserves and I found it most interesting.

But perhaps the high spot of my time in the U.S.S.R. was my stay at Askaniya Nova. The aim here is to cross domestic animals with wild related species and so improve the stock and, as well, to breed wild animals whose survival is in danger. The latter applies primarily to the Przevalsky horse.

The day after my arrival some of us set out with the Director to find the horses. Our small cart was pulled by a hybrid Przevalsky named Kapron, who jolted us along the steppe among herds of zebra, wildebeest, eland, stag, elk, moufflon, Watusi cattle, aurochs, water and Cape buffalo, Asian wild asses, llama, kongoni, impala and various other antelopes. I also observed zebroids, tiny Shetland ponies, dwarf stag from Indo-China and wapiti – it seemed as though the whole cargo of Noah's Ark had been unloaded here.

Towards the end of the day we came upon the Przevalsky herd which consisted of fourteen mares and one stallion, named Pegasus. These horses are very wild, they will not tolerate being handled and when they need to be shod have to be tranquillised by darting. We approached the herd on foot, scattering sheaves of maize to attract the mares who gradually drew near. Today there are only 210 Przevalsky horses in the world, of which fifteen are at Askaniya Nova. Another occasion for pride is that African eland antelopes have been bred here since 1892 and that the eland has been domesticated and even milked since 1948. My stay at Askaniya Nova was very stimulating, and when it was time for me to travel to Moscow I was sad. My last day in Russia was spent seventy-four miles north of Leningrad in a hunting reserve. Here I learned how very strictly hunting is controlled in the U.S.S.R., licences being required for shooting any important mammal and the number allowed to be killed by one gun in a season is small and related to the rarity of the animal.

Two years after my trip to Russia I was asked to go to Japan to meet people interested in establishing an Elsa Wild Life Appeal in their country. In Nara, famous for its temples, I saw the tame deer that roam the surrounding hills and was invited to their research station. In Mino, Japan's most ancient city, we discussed its sacred monkeys and then drove up into the hills till we reached

Monkey Heaven, the research centre for the *Macaca fuscate* monkeys. The warden told us that the research carried on over twenty-five years had been concentrated on three troops, totalling about sixty monkeys. The territory of a troop was around one square mile. The average life span of the monkeys had been thirty years but was now reduced to twenty-four, possibly because of the unsuitable food given to them by visitors despite the display of cautionary posters. The warden drew my attention to a curious fact; if the eyes of a human being look into those of an adult monkey the monkey panics and becomes aggressive but baby monkeys can look into a keeper's eyes with complete trust.

I was then flown to Hokkaido, Japan's most northerly island, to visit the Tancho Farm at Kushiro. Here research and breeding of the Japanese (Manchurian) crane is carried out. This is the largest of all cranes: with its white body, black wing and tail feathers and red cap it is also one of the most beautiful. Sadly the splendour of these stately birds became their death warrant; eventually their numbers were reduced to 140. Most of the killing happens during their migratory flights to the U.S.S.R. To prevent their extermination they are now being bred at the Tancho Farm, as well as in zoos. Later I saw a breeding pair at the Tokyo Zoo, their chick was reddish-brown and would only turn white when three months old.

Next morning I was taken to a national monument – this is the Japanese equivalent of a National Park. To my great surprise I saw settlements inside the area. I thought poaching might occur but was assured that the fines for poaching are too high to make it profitable and since there is not enough land available to set aside solely for the protection of wildlife, people live harmoniously side by side with the animals. There are no big predators in Japan (except for the bear that lives only in forests) which makes their coordination of human and animal interests possible.

Before leaving Japan I visited Mr Hata's Animal Kingdom at Hokkaido; he is a zoologist and author, and with the proceeds from his thirty-odd books has established a 270-square-mile research station to help to study wild and also domestic animals. Mr Hata is particularly well known for the book in which he describes how he lived for two years alone on an island with a brown bear who became a friend. We saw part of a film he had made at the time – it showed Mr Hata sharing the hibernation period with the bear who, even when half asleep, never lost his trust in his human companion.

From Japan I went on to Thailand where I had been invited by Mr Osot Kosin, an ardent naturalist. When he met me, as did some of the directors of Wildlife Sanctuaries and National Parks, I was surprised to hear that the film of *Born Free* was showing at Bangkok at that very moment. Mr Osot had arranged a wonderful tour for me, including a visit to his private sanctuary where I saw Indian spotted deer, barking deer, sambar deer, and two Thomson's gazelles which Mr Osot had bought during his last visit to Kenya. Next day Mrs Buri, a lady devoted to wildlife conservation and an adviser to the National Parks, took me to the Khao Yai National Park. On the way we called in at the animal market in Bangkok which was such an appalling sight that I offered to give funds from the Elsa Appeal, either to make it possible to employ inspectors or at least to print literature on the needs and treatment of wild animals. When we reached Khao Yai we were met by Dr Boonsong Lekagul, Thailand's most famous ornithologist and protector of wildlife, also several research students; I was asked to release one Pig-tail Macaque and a leopard-cat. All were locked up in boxes; opening the door to freedom for the monkey was easy but the leopard-cat gave me a good nip before dashing into a nearby thicket. When it was dark we went to the Park's hostel where Mrs Buri showed us a film on deforestation. One of the problems here is caused by opium growers. Since they know that their trade is illegal they uproot vast areas deep in the back of beyond in the hope that no one will find them there. Today, of course, they have to reckon with aerial control but even if they are discovered the damage is already done.

I was sorry when the time came to leave this enchanting country to fly back to Nairobi.

The humid climate of Japan had brought out latent arthritis in my pelvis and this rapidly increased; by now I was in pain most of the time. Moreover, to conform to traditional Japanese eating habits, I had while there to lower myself to the floor and arrange my legs crosswise underneath the low tables, smiling at the ever present cameras, even though I was in agonising pain. Luckily I completed the tour without collapsing. But on my return to Kenya I stepped almost directly from the plane into hospital, there to undergo a major operation on my hip. During the days of my convalescence I observed the wildlife at Elsamere and did some sketching but it was not long before I broke my right elbow which diminished still more the use of my hand. And I fractured my right knee as well . . .

During the two years it took me to recover from all these accidents, my patience was taxed to the maximum. Although the ever increasing work for the E.W.A.A. filled every hour of the day, I wanted to return to the bush and break new ground by studying a leopard.

To prepare for this, I investigated several National Parks to find a suitable location for the project and I broadcast the news that I was looking for a female leopard cub, but to no avail.

To increase my physical fitness I went for long walks into the hills near Elsamere. When I learned that the rare bongo antelope could still be found on one of the more remote hills, I made an expedition there with my friends, Ros and Bill Hylliar.

Bill had recently recovered from a major operation to his leg and therefore could not walk far, but he waited at a spring which we could reach by car. Struggling along a buffalo track through dense bamboo, Ros and I found fresh droppings and bongo spoor but they were far outnumbered by buffalo, whose traces we saw everywhere. After an hour's very steep walk we reached the top of the hill, but even there the forest was so thick that we could take no bearing of our position. We turned back, we presumed, on the buffalo track that we had come up – soon we realised we were mistaken. In our efforts to find the right track amongst so many that looked alike, we got lost. By then it was late afternoon so we began to hurry. Jumping over rotten logs and stones I fell and broke my right ankle. Inching myself down on my elbows and bottom I soon became sore, and worse still, was bitten by safari ants, an advancing column of which I had arrested with my posterior. I was beyond caring how painful their bites were, my only wish was to get to the bottom of the hill before dark, for the fresh spoor of buffalo all around left us in no doubt as to what our fate would be should we become benighted. The lower we descended, the more stinging nettles brushed against our legs. At last we reached level ground.

We had arrived at a swamp which was, we thought, close to the spring where Bill was waiting for us.

I had been able to slither down the steep buffalo track but I could not move across the swamp which, judging by the spoor, was a drinking place for buffaloes.

While waiting for Ros, who went off to find Bill, I had time to take in my situation. The temperature, at 7,000 feet, was already icy and if we had to spend the night here we would either die of exposure or be trampled by buffaloes. Shivering, I wondered if I should ever be able to cross the knee-deep swamp.

Even if Ros found Bill and Bill found me, it would take many hours to organise a rescue team. After some time, he did in fact appear – and with a Thermos of hot tea and a pullover, but I was horrified by his suggestion that he should carry me across the swamp for I knew that in his present condition any sudden effort might be fatal to him. He ignored my protests and finally we reached the car.

I was then driven straight to the Nairobi Hospital where we arrived at midnight. How could I ever thank my friends for having saved my life?

It was while in hospital I heard the tragic news of Billy Collins's sudden death due to a heart attack. Ever since I had met Sir William seventeen years ago, when I had shyly offered *Born Free* to Collins, we had become good friends and had published ten books together. He had not only always given me invaluable advice about the many problems of an inexperienced author but he had given ungrudging help in establishing the various Elsa Appeals, of which he was a Trustee.

Reflecting on the extraordinary events that had happened since the day we first met I realised that Elsa had become immortal; as for me I had spent a life (a life which was no longer my own) between the solitude of Kenya's bush and the bewildering jungle of large cities.

I had travelled across Africa, Asia, the U.S.A., Canada, Europe,

Australia, New Zealand and Japan speaking to people on behalf of endangered wildlife. I had received many high awards. Now I wondered how all this could have happened for I felt I had changed very little since the summer days at Seifenmühle when we children played at lion hunts. My ideas are the same as they have always been. For instance: I believe today as I did then that God is in every ray of sunshine, in the song of every bird, in the rustle of the wind; and the flicker of the setting sun, turning the country into gold, means more to me than any candle in a cathedral, and I still have no need to dress up to meet God on Sunday in a church for I can talk to him at any moment, as to my closest friend.

Back at Elsamere, I tried to assess the result of our efforts to preserve wildlife. Taking Kenya as an example, I found that poaching was still serious but that there were now 500 Wildlife Clubs which were doing splendid work among young Africans, who, a few years earlier, would have killed any wild animal on sight.

Among the many schemes the Elsa Wildlife Appeal and the Elsa Trust have helped are the establishment of Game Reserves at Meru, Samburu and Kora, the provision of a warden's house in the Shimba Hills National Park and firebreaks in Tsavo East National Park. Donations have been made to the Nairobi National Park's Veterinary Aid Fund and to the Flying Tuition Fund for National Park Game Wardens. But Elsa's help is of course not confined to Africa – it is worldwide. For instance, in Canada donations have been made for the preservation of wolves, kit-foxes, loons and also of urban wildlife, grants have been made to help to reduce the massacre of seals off the coasts of the United States and help has been given listing the birds of the remote Falkland Islands.

Working to help endangered species will, until the end of my life, be my main task but my immediate ambition was to study leopards. How to find a leopard cub was the problem.

At this moment, Lady Huxley arrived. She had come to Kenya to attend the thirtieth anniversary of UNESCO of which her husband, Sir Julian, had been Director General from 1946 to 1948. Ever since the Huxleys had visited Elsa's camp in 1969 we had become friends, so when the conference was over we visited a few National Parks.

At Lake Nakuru, towards sunet, we watched the pink of the flamingoes' feathers turn to red and contrast strikingly with the indigo of the hills. Fascinated by the scene, we were so busy taking photographs that we did not notice the ground getting softer and softer till suddenly the wheels of the car sank up to the hubs.

We collected driftwood, dry grasses, rags – even our shirts were sacrificed, but in spite of all our efforts the car went down deeper and deeper. Luckily, we were accompanied by two men who now decided to walk to the nearest ranger's post. Meanwhile, Lady Huxley and I remained in the car switching the headlights on and off to guide the hoped-for rescue party. We waited for three hours. When at last our friends returned with helpers, these included the ranger from the Park's headquarters and he gave me some thrilling news. At that very time, October 1976, he was looking after a one-month-old female leopard cub.

The cub is now in my care. From the moment of Penny's arrival, a new chapter in my life begins.

Appendix

Index